How To Travel Around The World
On A Backpacker's Budget

by
Dave Brett

Contents

Chapter One: Introduction.7
Chapter Two: Travel as a Lifestyle.9
Chapter Three: Mentality of a Backpacker.13
Chapter Four: Travelling Solo.18
Chapter Five: Budgeting.21
Chapter Six: Sell Your Junk.37
Chapter Seven: Philosophy of Packing.45
Chapter Eight: Three Important Items. 52
Chapter Nine: Clothing.67
Chapter Ten: Hygiene.79
Chapter Eleven: Technology.85
Chapter Twelve: Optional Items.94
Chapter Thirteen: The Art of Packing Light.99
Chapter Fourteen: Transportation.108
Chapter fifteen: Booking Flights Like A Travel Ninja.109
Chapter Sixteen: Around the World Tickets (RTW).127
Chapter Seventeen: Flying Tips.138
Chapter Eighteen: Train Tricks and Rail Passes.146
Chapter Nineteen: Bus About.154
Chapter Twenty: Driving Around.156
Chapter Twenty One: Accommodation.159
Chapter Twenty Two: Hostels.163
Chapter Twenty Three: Hotels.175
Chapter Twenty Four: Alternative Sleeps.178
Chapter Twenty Five: House Share.185
Chapter Twenty Six: Home Hospitality.190
Chapter Twenty Seven: Food for Thought.204
Chapter Twenty Eight: Visa Information.212
Chapter Twenty Nine: Travel Insurance. 215
Chapter Thirty: Health.221
Chapter Thirty One: A world of Work & Study.224
Chapter Thirty Two: Wrapping it up.240

This book is dedicated to all those who have helped me along my journey.

Chapter One: Introduction

With a little bit of planning and preparation it's very possible for anyone to travel the world.

That's where I got the idea for this book. if you think that long-term global travel is limited to just rich millionaires, then you are by far very mistaken. Sure, you won't be travelling first class and staying in 5 star accommodations, but you will be experiencing the same exciting cultural wonders that the world has to offer.

Don't take it from me, just head to any hostel anywhere around the world and you'll instantly meet many people who are currently travelling right now, all very differently, but they are all doing it. It's never been easier to explore the world due to the Internet, which has made travel more affordable and more connected.

Armed with this travelling knowledge, use it wisely to improve yourself and make the most of exploring the larger world around you.

I've broken up this book into easy to follow sections to get you prepared for a world of travel. You will mostly learn as you go along, but this book will hook you up with the core basics needed to get you started. Feel free to dip in and out, skip sections and come back to chapters at any time you wish, This is your book to shape how you wish to travel.

Chapter Two: Travel as a Lifestyle

Travel is not a religion, but choosing a life focused on travelling is a lifestyle choice that you can make. We all have passions and hobbies and it's important to have our own unique interests and that's what makes us who we are. I choose travel and all of my income and finances go towards funding this lifestyle. Just like someone who has an interest in Star Wars Movies or following a Football club, the passion I support is travel. This drive and determination to travel more and to see the world as my number one priority helps me to make it happen.

What's the difference between taking one year out of your life after college or university to not taking that gap year at all? Think about it; you will end up working in the same job till retirement age, but now you will have to work an extra year. When you're ready for retirement do you think you will be annoyed that you spent an extra year of your youth travelling around the world? Do you think you will be disappointed that whilst everyone around you is retiring, you will have to work an extra year that you took out for some travelling in your youth?

It most probably will be the one year of your life you most remember; The one that shaped your philosophy for life and gave you a firm foundation and knowledge of the world. It will be the one year you think 'wow what a life that was, weren't all those amazing experiences incredible?' You will return to normal life full of fire and ready to go. Full of life and wanting more. You most probably picked up a lot of real life experiences on your year out as well.

One year out of your normal life will not affect your future negatively, In fact it might benefit positively. imagine going for a job interview armed with a year of travelling experience? This might put you one step ahead of your competitors going for the same job.

You will see life in the 3rd world first hand and get to understand poverty on a personal level. When countries pop up on the news that you might have visited you will understand the situation a lot more than the person sitting next to you. When you see a lost Australian in London, you will cast your mind back to the moment when a helpful Australian helped you out with a map when you were lost in Sydney, and you'll want to help the troubled backpacker out.

The one thing that makes us not travel full time is based on two elements:

You either have all the time in the world but no money, or you have all the money in the world but no time to use it.

You need to discover the correct balance.

The easiest answer is to travel the world with lots of free time but with no money. I'm not suggesting that you should become homeless and live in a cardboard box. Simply what do you value more? Working for money, or having more time to enjoy life? Working out the balance of living with little money as possible, helps free up time to travel and allows you to pursue this lifestyle.

When you're willing to put everything on the line to do something you love, you're happy to rough it in order to make it possible. You can limit your spending by cutting out a lot and focusing on the one thing you want to fund.

Chapter Three: Mentality of a Backpacker

Fear is one of the big reasons that puts people off from travelling. It may look like a scary world out there but your normally find more friendly faces. Your quickly discover that the negative travel related news stories will spread like wildfire rather than the good experiences. These situations rarely happen and they shouldn't put you off travelling. It is sad when backpackers die in a bus crash in South America. But every day millions of backpackers are moving constantly all around the world. You don't hear about how successful their journey went, as it's not interesting, so don't let the negative news put you off.

Some people relate travel to being a very stressful, unsafe experience, especially when you're planning it yourself, but this doesn't have to be the case.

Let travel take over your life and enjoy it

Being organised can make a big difference but you don't want to be completely taken over by it. Booking your whole trip at once will not allow room for flexibility and that's what you want in order to experience the joys of travelling, freedom. Travelling for the first time will make you want to book everything in advance as you're heading into the unknown and want everything to be perfect. That's understandable as you don't want to miss out on all the wonderful things travel can offer. But this doubt can cause you a lot of problems in the future when you will demand more flexibility, and flexibility is something you won't have if you're locked into all your bookings.

But that's exactly the point, booking everything will make you want to do everything and you're going to wear yourself out and you'll end up hating travelling. What you want to do is spread it out and go with the flow, that's truly the best travel experience you can plan for. Have a rough plan but do as you want in between. Leave your stressed out life at home and be happy to have the spare time to do whatever you want, make the most of it. You'll meet fun people that might be going a different route and you can easily change yours if you don't have any bookings.

One aspect you will have to book in advance will be flights; the simple reason for this is because booking them on the day can cost you a fortune. Advance booking will help you to cut the cost of your trip. So allow some space between the two dates and then worry about them when they come along.

Also, keep an eye out for key dates such as festivals/major sporting events/public holidays that might be happening in the location you're going to visit, you don't want to arrive a day before and everything is fully booked.

I like to book my first hotel/hostel on arrival, it helps with filling out your visa information for the location and after a long flight the last thing you want is a 4 hour trek around a city to find a place to stay. The next day you wake up you can then do as you wish.

You may also book some selected tours, some areas of your travel have to be booked in advance, so book them now. For example, the Inca trail to Machu Picchu needs advance booking, you can't just turn up and join a tour (well you can, but this is highly illegal and you don't want to get into trouble). So for these areas you should book, but leave the rest to the 'going with the flow' spirit.

Information is key

Avoid being a part of scams or tourist traps by reading up on some local knowledge in a guide book. I like to purchase the Lonely Planet guide book for each destination on my Amazon Kindle. Another alternative is to use www.wikitravel.org which is free and you can print or download onto a PDF. You quickly pick up some local history and information on where you are visiting which is helpful to understand the people, as well as reading up on the warnings which you should know about before you arrive. This information alone is well worth the cover price of the Amazon kindle guidebook and you can easily read all this on the flight over before you arrive so you're fully up-to-date.

It's also wise to read about the customs and what you should do to prepare yourself so you avoid not offending anyone. For example, in my Lonely Planet guidebook it informed me Malaysia has a lot of religious areas which should be respected and you should cover up when visiting these areas and generally when walking around cities, I had no idea before visiting and this is smart information. It's just important to pick these tips up as you won't be told them when you arrive, you will just be expected to know them and this can easily offend locals which is never a good thing. Read up on the location before you arrive and you can keep on top of these areas and continue to be a well informed traveller.

Chapter Four: Travelling Solo

The best form of travelling is by yourself, and I swear by it. When you're on your own people will approach you more easily to talk to. This helps, because if you travel as a couple or with friends you'll be building a bubble around you that will put people off from talking to you. Travelling on your own can be fun as you put more effort into meeting new people on your travels and you'll be constantly making new contacts and creating new friends.

Travelling on your own will give you the chance to fully understand yourself as a person as you have to quickly adapt and learn in new surroundings. You'll also be able to decide what you want to do and avoid doing a lot of things you have no interest in. If you want to go to a Manga convention on your visit to Kyoto you can! It's your life, your journey and it's your money, so everything is down to you to do whatever you want to do and that's amazing.

You overslept and missed your train, who cares? No one will know about it but you, just wake up and get the next one. The freedom of travelling solo. I admit, it will be lonely at some points of your trip but there is nothing stopping you from meeting and making new friends along the way at hostels or on Couchsurfing.

Spending time with yourself on such big trips can be a real personal builder for your self-development and you learn about yourself very quickly. Travelling by yourself is a great independence and confidence builder. Don't be afraid to go alone, no one is telling you that you have to go with someone.

Travelling with a friend or group can cause a lot of trouble for your trip and really damage it in a way, as you have to constantly decide together what you want to do next and where you will stay. You have to be very careful when deciding to travel with someone because you will be spending in some cases a whole year with them; do you really trust that person enough to travel with them? If you're on your own you cut out a lot of this time wasting and will just naturally go with the flow and you can do what you truly want to do.

Chapter Five: Budgeting

A rough budget for an around the world trip for a year (gap year) roughly works out in the region of £10,000. Of course this depends on how you're moving around and where about you'll be visiting, but that's a rough estimate to aim towards.

If you want to spend most of your time in Australia and New Zealand you will want to take extra or you could blend your trip with a working visa and earn whilst you're travelling to top up your budget.

Working whilst travelling will help you to travel quicker and if you have cash already from selling all your stuff and just want to go now, then you can. Why work in a bar in London when you could work in a bar in Australia and experience living abroad whilst you're earning? Not only this; but the wages in

Australia at the moment (2014) are much higher and work is in more demand in the hospitality sector in comparison to the UK.

Then after you have earned cash in Australia you can travel around a cheaper destination such as Vietnam or Cambodia with your earnings which is totally possible. If you travel to Australia at the moment and decide not work, you could be in for a shock as the prices are very high. If you earn and travel it's not as bad as the minimum wage is rather high for Brits at the moment and this could be a good way of doing it.

I could tell you to work in a bar or an office in the UK for a year to raise enough funds towards your travels, but if you can sell your junk and set yourself a goal to raise around £3,000 (which you need in your account to enter Australia on a working visa) whilst working over a couple of months, then you can book your RTW (Round the World) flight via Australia and you're away. Save the money up in another country it's far more exciting.

You will not only earn money in Australia, but get an early taste of travelling and it will shape and prepare you for the rest of the world. Australia is a great first time destination because the language and culture are very similar to the UK, but it's half way across the planet, so you have escaped your family and motherland enough for it to be an awesome learning experience.

Canada and New Zealand can also be noted for this same reason, but Australia is far more use to hosting first time travels which makes it more easier to adapt. For more information about the working holiday visa for Australia you can read about this in the Visa section of this book.

Heading to expensive destinations can really blow a hole in your wallet, stick to more affordable not so popular destinations such as Cambodia. Not only will you save a lot of money it will be more of an adventure as well.

Setting yourself a monthly limit for each destination can really help your money situation. Stick to your budget and avoid spending it all at once. Money management is a good thing when you're travelling as you can easily spend it in the wrong areas. Going broke on your travels is not an option and is a horrible experience. Phoning your parents can be seen as a defeat and the last thing you would ever want to do, so stop yourself from getting into this hole. Also, who said your parents are willing to help you out? Exactly, so avoid this situation.

The best way to look at your travelling budget is using your money to get the most out of it. One beer here is a beach hut there, what do you value the most? Just because everyone else is partying every day doesn't mean you have to. Stick to your limits, understand why you have limits and respect it.

Your money is your money and not others so do what you want to do with it and don't be pushed into peer pressure, it's ok to say no. At the same time it's important to breathe and having too much of a restricted budget can take away the joy of travelling, so make sure you don't struggle too much and discover the correct balance for you.

What I normally do is have a pot of money in my saving account called the 'fun pot'. When you stumble across one of these 'once in a lifetime' experiences, to miss it would just be a crime in itself. This is when you should splash out and use this tucked away fund. If your planned monthly budget works out to be too much for what you needed, you can always put the remaining budget in this fund to come back to when you want to do something really fun but it's not in your budget. Try and do this once a month, but not too often so you get the most out of the experience. You can also use this as an emergency fund if worse comes to worse.

It's important to understand the value of money, getting your budget spot on can help you see more and help you to avoid spending it all at once, which can be way too easy when given the opportunity. Just imagine how happy your future self will be in the next continent knowing that you thought about them and left them allocated budget to play with rather than splashing it all on a week straight bender of beer in Singapore. Be smart and you'll travel far.

Budget by Continent

Having a comfortable budget for each area means comfortable travel, so level it out and play with it a little when you arrive to make sure it fits your budget and your destination. You want to divide your money into a weekly budget based on the destinations you're visiting. You need more money in Australia than you will in Thailand, so make sure you get the balance right or it could all go terribly wrong. I've laid out what to expect, finance-wise, in each location. Here is a rundown of how much you might need in each area of the world destinations:

South East Asia

Daily Budget: £10

A very popular destination for backpackers, because of the low cost of living, you can literally live like a king on £400 a month. With nice places to stay and eating out every day as well as travelling by luxury sleeper bus. If done smartly it's actually possible to live off £200 for the month in some areas, if you use cheap guest houses and only eat street food.

Daily budget is based on comfortable living which includes local transport, 3 meals and drinks, place to stay (budget is cut if using home hospitality) as well as a little spending for affordable attractions.

India

Daily Budget: £10

Cheap transportation by train and lots of affordable guest houses. Food is incredible for the value as well, vegetarian food in India is amongst the best in the world and very affordable so make the most out of it.

China (outside of big cities ie. Beijing/Shanghai)

Daily Budget: £25

Expensive to get to, but cheap once you are there. Guest houses are very affordable, domestic transport can be expensive with the introduction of new speed trains which can cost a lot

Japan

Daily Budget: £40

Can be very expensive due to accommodation, but plenty of 100 yen shops to find affordable food and with the Japan rail pass transport can be affordable. It's just the price of the accommodation that can be a drawback unless you sleep in pod hotels or internet cafes.

Europe

Daily Budget: £20 for East/ £30 for central and £40 for North region (plus UK/Ireland)

Northern and central Europe can be very expensive but sticking to more affordable destinations such as Czech Republic, Slovakia, Estonia, Latvia, Lithuania, Poland, and other areas in Eastern Europe, you will find that the food is very affordable. Also, hostels are easily located in the major cities as well as low cost trains and buses. A one day budget in Oslo could stretch a whole week in Bulgaria so make sure you spend your budget in the correct areas.

Central America

Daily Budget: £15

Mexico to Panama is great for low cost backpacking as they have lots of cheap chicken buses on offer and hostels are affordable too. The street food tends to be very low cost as well and it won't set you back that much for a nice meal and drink in a restaurant (about £4). It's a fun place to explore with lots of Mayan ruins and white sand beaches.

Australia and New Zealand

Daily Budget: £40

Can be very expensive with regards to food and accommodation and will limit how long you wish to stay there. However, applying for a working visa and earning Australian or New Zealand dollars is a smart move at the moment as they pay quite well, so you will be able to afford to live there on the local salary. It's a good destination to save up travel funds for other destinations such as South East Asia. Why work at home when you can have fun doing it down under while the AUS dollar is doing well at the moment; it's a win-win!

Africa

Daily Budget: £20-30

Can be very expensive due to flights getting there and accommodation is not popular, so tourism options are low. However, food and drink is very cheap, bare in mind you pretty much have to pay for visas everywhere so it can be expensive to hop around the different countries.

Using your personal budget along with the Daily recommendation for each destination, you can work out how long you can stay in each area. Keeping expensive destinations at the start rather than the end of your trip will help you out in the future. It's better to be skint in an affordable country than an expensive one, because its just a slight change of lifestyle you will have to adapt to. Being broke in an expensive country can cause a lot of problems and could turn into a disaster.

Money exchange

It's important to get your finances into gear so you can keep track of your spending, one area is to make sure that your money doesn't get wasted easily from terrible exchange rates, luckily I have a few tips on how to avoid this.

Money is sometimes overlooked as a way of making your trip go longer. You most probably have sold all of your stuff by now and worked your ass off in a bar (be it London or Sydney) to pay for the rest of the trip, so why chuck it down the drain? Shopping around for the best exchange rate can be a good deal if you grab the right price. Depending on the amount that you're going to spend, shopping around can save you around £10 per trip or even over £100+ for a whole gap year.

It might not seem a lot but over time it can add up and also it only took me 30 minutes to shop around on the high street and on the internet to find a better deal, time that's totally worth it.

Rule number one: Don't exchange at the airport!

Commission free does not mean that you're getting a good exchange, they still can sting you on the exchange rate so bare this in mind. Airports are not the best places to pick up a deal as the environment makes it harder to compare the daily exchange rate, so they tend to charge a premium as a result.

To check the daily exchange I like to use www.xe.com and they have a fantastic application for the iPhone/iPad that works both on and offline. This will give you a rough estimate of what you should be working towards so you don't get completely mugged off.

How about withdrawing at the ATM?

For some this can be a good option, but again the bank specifies the exchange rate by themselves making it not terribly competitive. Some cards will not charge you to take out cash abroad and offer a good exchange rate. Search around the internet for these types of cards in your country. In the UK you can have a look at these cards on www.moneysavingexpert.com. One example at the moment is the Halifax Clarity card which offers no charges on international withdrawals, perfect.

Countries such as the UK, Finland & Singapore widely accept debit card micro payments such as €1 for a coffee. However, for countries such as Russia, taking your rubbles out in advance can save the pennies where it matters.

For larger amounts, make your money go further. Shop around, most high streets up and down the country will have places that offer currency exchanges. Hop around and take photos of the exchange boards and see what you can find.

Places to consider in the UK:

Royal Mail Post Office, Marks and Spencer's, travel agents, major super markets and your personal bank.

Some might offer special bulk deals if you take out £500 or more, see if this works for you and if you're going with a friend on your trip see if they want to split 50/50 to save on a bulk deal. Some local banks are now doing it online so investigate if your bank is now offering this service. Once you have wandered around your high street and captured all the deals (online as well) see which has the best offer on the day.

By doing all the following steps you are able to work out what the best deal is for you on the day and it will be a much better step than taking it out at the airport. The above works well for US dollars, euros and other popular currencies, but if you're going to a more unique currency destination maybe it's better to haggle when you get there and take out a small amount before you take your trip for emergency purposes.

I hope the above works and remember; you have earned the money hard and fare, so make it work that little extra. There are loads of people that would happily take your money, so work with it and get the best deal for your trip. Imagine all the wonderful tasty street food you can now purchase with your savings.

First of all it's very important to inform your bank that you're going to be travelling abroad as they will cut off your access quicker than a heartbeat. Believe me; it's happened to me enough times for it not to happen again. It only takes a quick simple call; give them some destinations and dates and you're sorted for the rest of your trip. This also helps with fraud so if anything does happen to your account whilst overseas they are aware that you're travelling and can act accordingly.

Next you want to capture digital copies of your credit cards in case they get lost (along with all your other documents as previously discussed). You can secure them safely online within your email account. Then at least if your wallet gets stolen, you still have some form of back up.

It's also a good idea to spread your money and credit cards around, some in your pocket, some in your bag. Just in case one gets lost or stolen, you will still have the other as a backup.

Chapter Six: Sell Your Junk

Sometimes you have to get creative. There are lots of ways to make money on the internet; some crazier than others to fund your travels.

Make money from your junk

Right now you own a lot of crap. You may not look at it as crap, but if one thing is for sure, it's holding you down. Clutter is one of the biggest drags in life. Why should you let the things you own, take over your life? Owning things you don't need costs you a lot – it costs you to buy them in the first place and it costs you to store it. But what if I tell you you're sitting on a gold mine? One man's junk is another man's treasure (people will buy anything on the internet!).

I enjoy looking at the Sahara nomads that travel across dunes and live in tents. All they have is camels and what they can fit on them. If it doesn't fit, they don't take it – it's as simple as that! They simply pack for a purpose and for survival and not for convenience or comfort. What you're doing is taking this concept and turning it digital. The digital nomad is born. All you're doing is taking the nomadic concept and applying it to a more digital updated version for global travel.

One great idea to make quick and easy cash, apart from working, is to sell what you already have. Over the years you have accumulated a lot of stuff and the majority of it you hardly use enough to get any use out of it, or you simply don't use it at all. Just look around you and ask yourself which items do you use every day and which items could you live without.

When you're travelling you no longer require most of this stuff. Stop having an attachment to your toaster and turn it into some cash. You're living a nomadic lifestyle now. When you finally need a toaster in the future buy it, but right now you don't need it so don't waste money storing it and sell it to make some much needed travelling funds.

One way to look at it, if your house is burning down and you only have 5 minutes to grab what you can, what items would they be and why? Making you think in this way truly makes you think about what you value and what can't be replaced. Use this time wisely to go through all of your stuff and feel lucky that your house isn't burning down, as now you can finally sort out what you value the most and cut down on your clutter. Remember, no one ever grabs the TV!

The past 9 years of my life, I have never owned a TV. I have been very grateful for the experience, I now prefer my lifestyle without it. If there is a program that everyone is talking about, I'll download it and watch it where I want, when I want. News is another great example of why you don't need a TV. You can follow news on Twitter and just read the news you want to read about in more depth by following the tweet URL to the video/article. This is surely better than tuning in every day at the same time to watch a show that someone else has put together based on a general opinion of what's popular. You're in control of your life and you're now saving a lot of time using this method.

TV has become more advanced by the year and yours will be out of date soon before you know it, not only this, but you can just go down the street and buy a new one very easily and most probably your home insurance covers fire damage on TV so why would you grab the TV? Exactly! Get rid of it! Use that money to see the Sahara Desert rather than watching it on the Discovery channel. Selling your possessions will fund a nice weeklong stay somewhere or a handful of budget airline flights.

Sell your Playstation, get some money for it. It's not going to be doing any good sitting in storage and collecting dust. Because one thing is for sure, you won't be able to take it with you on your travels. When you return from your travels and you miss your Playstation, just buy a new one (most probably a newer version as well!) Use the money to do something exciting like a bungee jump, isn't that more exciting than playing a game at home?

If you're going to rent your apartment out to a lodger, or stop renting somewhere in order to travel, then you're going to end up with a lot of stuff. Turn this unneeded junk into hard cash that you can use on your travels. Mentally imagine every DVD you have as a night in a Cambodian guest house or a beer in Australia, use your stuff as travel vouchers and help you travel further. The stuff you want to keep will cost you a lot of money in storage lockers so avoid this unneeded cost and chuck the lot!

Movies, music and books take up a lot of space; turn them into digital format by selling them and buying the digital version. You can then store them online in the cloud or store them on a hard drive. This is the way you should be thinking when living a nomadic lifestyle.

For quick media sales in the UK you could use www.musicmagpie.co.uk. You won't get a lot of money compared to www.ebay.co.uk but it's quick and easy to get a quote so if you have a large collection this could be a better option to flog the lot.

For un-used clothes many websites buy bulk fabric so you can see if they do a collect option, they buy your clothes depending on weight, again a quick sale and you won't get a lot but better than nothing.

One example: www.cash-clothes.co.uk/sell-old-clothes

Can't sell it, or don't want it? Do some good and send it off to the charity shop. At least your junk can find a good home and support something good along the way.

Sell as much as you can or send it off to the charity shop, you will have some items you will find hard to depart with but this really should be the last resort.

Really try hard to flog the lot off and de-clutter your life. Stuff you can't depart with such as school photos, etc. ask your parents if you can use a small amount of storage space - normally they will be happy to help out with such items and it saves you having to put it into storage. Avoid storage at all costs as it's going to cut into your monthly budget. You really can get rid of a lot of stuff so use this opportunity wisely!

Putting your whole life into one bag is not an easy task, but it's totally possible. With your new travelling lifestyle you no longer need a lot of junk - so get rid of it! You can actually see many examples of this on YouTube of people travelling the world with everything they own on the planet in one small hand luggage bag.

You will have nothing to worry about apart from your hand luggage. You will be very free as you can hop, skip or jump freely where ever you want, without having to worry about everything you own, as it's all in one small mobile bag.

Biggest two advantages:

A. Can check-in just hand luggage

B. Never have to worry about a house to store all your things.

Clutter-free lifestyle, it's great for the mind and great for you. No longer are you weighed down by junk you really don't need in your life.

Chapter Seven: Philosophy of Packing

Space is your friend but just because you have it doesn't mean it needs to be filled.

I ditched a lot of stuff as I went along. I remember having a gear haul half way through my trip and I said to myself that if I wasn't using it on a weekly basis it had to go. Shockingly some things in my bag I hadn't even used at all and some items maybe only once or twice.

It's a tricky world packing for the unexpected, but really all you need are the basics you use in your usual daily life.

Getting this part right can help you dramatically when you're travelling. The last thing you want to do is to be weighed down with baggage. You want to be free after all, isn't that the joy of travelling! Minimalist thinking can help you towards the path of living like a digital nomad.

Digital nomads work with a laptop and a bag with all their worldly possessions in it. This forces digital nomads to create a lifestyle where they are completely mobile and location independent.

For a beginner it's not going to be easy to instantly pack like a traveller who has been doing it for several years. However, I'm here to guide you through the process of how I prepare my bag for global travel. I will reveal exactly what I pack and how I pack it.

At first, it might seem like you are packing for the apocalypse. You're thinking in an over prepared state and want to pack everything, this is natural. It's one of the scariest aspects when leaving your comfort zone for the first time and there is no shame in that. But the number one rule of packing light is, buy it when you get there. You no longer have to pack the way you always have, it may seem like mission impossible now, but I hope I can explain how to pack for an extended amount of time, which is a completely different way of packing.

You're going to become better at packing once you get into a rhythm and stick at it. It's something you become better at over time.

"Take half your baggage and double your money"

Every time I read this frequent quote from how-to-travel books, it makes me cringe. How does that person know exactly what you have packed? Also, if you could tell me an easy way to double my money, I would love to hear it. Rather than giving you a large list of items and then telling you to get it, I want to tell you the bare basics of what you need to pack and you can then build around that.

It's a sort of Maslow's hierarchy of needs, but relating to packing for long term travel. I'll give you a list of the most important items I feel would be uncomfortable to travel without, then you can work out the rest relating to what you value the most.

I've just listed the exact minimum required to live a nomadic lifestyle out of a hand luggage sized bag. Anything else you want to add is up to you. If you value an item a lot, then who am I to say don't pack it? But be warned; please don't go overboard.

Another clearer example of this is photography equipment. If your whole life is focused around photography, then me telling you to live with Instagram using a smart phone is not going to help. Take the things you value the most if they will enhance your trip in a dramatic way; such as improving your photography skills and selling the pictures as you travel. In this case you will need to take your equipment and maybe an extra photography bag (Lens, tripods ect). Bottom line, as long as you respect the minimum approach, then you will thank me in the long run when you have an extremely light pack.

I hope by now you're in the correct mindset, packing something of high value will stop you from packing something not so important. As long as you're prepared to take this on board then you understand the value of packing.

I could give you a list of items people frequently travel with, but I would feel that I was lying to you. Yes, I would say a majority of these items many travellers do purchase and travel with. But I can also tell you that the more experienced backpackers soon drop them after a while into a trash can. It's not until you're finally on the road when you start to discover what you value the most, that's why I want to inform you that this is a very different way of packing. It's come from many years of travelling and learning the hard way.

I once was in your shoes and wasted allot of money on gear, items I soon discarded in order to make my bag lighter and easier to travel with. Once you're travelling it's hard to dump items you have spent allot of money on, you form an emotional attachment which is hard to break out of. That's why I want you to get it right from the start so you can avoid making the same mistake. Instead spend the money in the correct areas and avoid taking what you don't have to.

The bare minimum you need to pack in order to travel.

The prospect of packing your whole life into one small hand luggage might seem daunting and next to impossible. But it's the best travelling advice I can offer to any first time traveller. When you have hand luggage, you won't be weighed down and constantly worrying about storage and the safety of your belongings.

Advantages of travelling with just hand luggage:

- Save on check-in baggage fees
- Avoid checks-in desks and check-in online
- Save money on taxis that charge for baggage
- Save money on locker fees

- Be less of a target and look more like a local
- Take up less space when staying with a couch surfer
- Less back pain
- Be able to pack and go within no time
- Extremely mobile

Chapter Eight: Three Important Items

Items you must not skimp on:

- Bag
- Shoes
- Water proof jacket

If there were 3 items that I would not recommend cutting corners on, it would be these three items. If you want to splash your money on something, then this is the area you should look into doing so.

Bag

The way you should look at your bag is the same way a turtle wears a shell, it's going to be your new home. So choose wisely, you want it to be as comfortable as possible. Buying a cheap or fake branded backpack is really going to make you suffer in the long run. It's going to be uncomfortable, back-breaking and it will fall apart at the seams half way through your trip. Whatever you do, don't cut corners on the bag!

A bag is for life, not just for one trip.

Tips when buying: Between 30-40 litres capacity, carry 10kg comfortably and with maximum dimensions of 55cmx40cmx20cm. This guideline is frequently found in the information given to you by airlines for check-in luggage.

How to choose the best bag? My advice is to go along to your local outdoor centre that sells outdoor equipment. Here are some examples of stores I recommend around the globe:

United Kingdom:

Blacks: www.blacks.co.uk

Ellis Brigham: www.ellis-brigham.com

Cotswold: www.cotswoldoutdoor.com

Field and trek: www.fieldandtrek.com

Australia/New Zealand:

Kathmandu: www.kathmandu.com.au

USA:

REI: www.rei.com

Canada:

MEC: www.mec.ca

Online Worldwide backpacks worth also checking out:

Minaal: http://www.minaal.com/ks-get-your-bag/

Tombihn: http://www.tombihn.com

Just a note; I have both visited and purchased items from all of the above stores, so am happy to vouch for them.

So why have I told you to go to these stores?

Not only will you receive expert advice, you can try on the bags for yourself which you can't do online. When you go to these stores, you will be welcomed by a member of staff who has done a fair bit of travelling themselves and will possibly offer their expert opinion on the product you're looking at. Not only this, but once you try on the product then you can best find out if the product fits your body-frame. Everyone has a different frame so not all bags will suit everyone.

Another point is the above stores will have measuring sticks to measure the top of your back to the bottom. This will help you find the type of frame that you are, and what size of bag will be most suitable. They also tend to have Bean bag weights that they can put in your bag, so you can feel what it's going to be like when it's fully loaded.

Things I like to look out for with a good bag:

Waterproof pullover that's built in. This helps to keep your bag dry when it rains and allows you to cut out an umbrella.

Compression straps to pull out unneeded air from your bag and makes it more compact.

Good waist support strap that can be tucked away when not in use.

Good chest clip to give you upper body support. Built in whistle is a bonus.

Padded laptop compartment for extra security.

Lots of storage pockets for cables and passports and pens ECT, helps with organization.

Front easy grab pocket for things like chewing gum and sunglasses

Outside water bottle holder.

With all the above knowledge, you will be able to walk into an outdoor store and look at the bag that fits the most requirements, but most importantly, fits you the best.

My recommendation?

The North Face - Surge backpack

Shoes

This comes down to individual choice, but a very important choice to make as well. Your chosen shoes are going to be made to work there soles off because when a lot of globe-trotting is involved, you're going to need some rugged footwear to get you from A to

B. On average my walking increases dramatically when I travel, as I often avoid public transport as much as possible and walk around on foot. Plus, with all the lovely scenery to explore, you're simply going to be walking a lot compared to normal. The terrain is going to change dramatically and will really push your footwear to the max compared to back home where it mostly stays the same.

I've heard stories of some backpackers going through several pairs of shoes on their travels but the large majority of us will just need to research and invest wisely in one pair to do the trick.

Sports trainers

Yep, for some weird reason they just work with travelling, they can fold into themselves and can be strapped onto the side of your bag when your flip flopping around and you can also use them for running and sports which is a double bonus. But that's it; a simple pair of trainers will do the job very well. I like to buy a more casual dark coloured pair just to give me more of a chance to get into a nightclub as packing black shoes is impossible and out of the question. But they are rugged enough to cover a lot of basic backpacking situations, so go with this option. Have a look at what's out there and pick a pair that's comfortable.

Do invest in some good solid footwear, a good rugged quality that will withstand the test of time. You're going to be walking a lot of miles, so don't cut corners here. Don't take a cheaper option and do shop around, they will get used, trust me. Just a travel tip; make sure that you wear your shoes in a month before your trip, so your feet can adjust to them before the terrain changes.

Another brand to look out for is Vibram, you can find them built into many popular sports trainer soles. Vibram is a good make to look out as they offer a high level of protection between the ground and your feet, perfect for mountain walking and hard surfaces. Gore-tex can also be found in outdoor trainers if you wanted to protect yourself from the elements.

My recommendation?

The North Face Hedgehog GTX XCR III

Additional Flip-flops

Flip-flops are a must for backpackers as they not only double up as indoor shoes, you can use them in the showers at hostels and in hot climates where shoes are uncomfortable. They are flat and easy to pack which is an added bonus; this means you can take them in addition to your one pair of shoes. I have invested in a nice pair of Havana's, which are like the tanks of flip-flops. If you're travelling to South America, you can pick them up rather cheap in comparison to Europe. I've had my pair for 7 years now and they're still going great!

No boots?

Don't travellers use boots? I thought you were going to say boots? A common stereotype is that backpackers wear boots, but I'm here to tell you that I've never taken boots on my travels. If you plan on just hiking the whole time then you most probably will want to skip the trainers and just wear boots. No problems with that, but never take both as boots take up so much space. If you do however plan on doing some hiking, but not frequently, there is no point lugging big bulky hiking boots around the world when you're not going to be using them every day.

My advice is to rent them when you need them. When I was hiking around some New Zealand glaciers, (the only time on the trip when I needed boots) I was able to rent them from the hiking centre. The amount of the rental cost worked out better than buying a pair of my own and then lugging them around the world.

Simply put; you can travel around the world with one good pair of flip-flops and one pair of trainers.

Waterproof jacket

Don't buy a cheap one!

Cheap rain jackets are not built for long term travelling. You're going to be hitting some pretty rainy destinations, whether you like it or not, and unexpected in most cases as well. Sure you can buy a cheap $1 poncho when travelling around Cambodia but if you're visiting Bergen for the weekend, you want something that can withstand the forces of nature. It doesn't have to be too technical either, just something of quality that's going to work and last.

My tip is to buy a light shell; anything too bulky takes up a lot of space. Yes a bulky jacket is warm, but you can use a fleece as an under layer with a light shell and still get the same result. I use this method so that I can pack as little as possible, as creating a layering system makes laundry easy. Layers can be taken off and on, bulky jackets do not have this feature which makes it hard to manage your clothing in your bag. I'll talk a bit more about the fleece on the next page but at the moment a good light rain jacket shell will do the trick. Again you can ask the sales assistant in the store when getting your bag and shoes if there is anything they recommend. You can buy jackets with built in layering systems, where the fleece zips into the jacket in order to create a hybrid product.

Personally I'm a big fan of Gore-Tex, which is a type of waterproofing that comes with many good jackets. Normally when you go along with this brand you're guaranteed to keep dry.

My recommendation?

The North Face - Point Five Jacket

Tips for the Outdoor store

It's a good idea to set aside a whole day of research to shop for the above three items, either online or at the high street. Then you can seek out the best product at the best price to suit you. Now you can do one of three things:

1) If you're happy with the price and the service from the store, buy the product. Don't forget to ask if they do any type of discount such as membership/student discount, this might save you some much needed cash and you only have to ask.

2) If a birthday or Christmas is coming up, you can always ask if it could be gifted to you. This is something you're going to have for a lifetime and use every day and would make a perfect gift.

3) Have a search online to see if you can find the item cheaper. You can try a number of sites such as eBay, Amazon, Hukd or Google shopping search.

4) If you have time, wait for the sales to come around and try your luck.

It's best to shop around as saving any type of money helps towards the funding of your trip and helping you towards choosing the perfect gear that suits you.

In the end if you are happy with the service of the store, go with them, simple.

Chapter Nine: Clothing

Next you're going to want to sort out your clothing. Now this might come across as rather extreme compared to your current wardrobe but I'm deadly serious, we have to get your life into a hand luggage sized bag.

Base layer:

The 5x5x5 Base layer rule:

5 x T-Shirts

5 x Underwear

5 x Socks

These are the most important items you need in order to not be naked. Now that's important! I've found that 5 of each is enough to withstand a weekly laundry wash and works really well. Wearing one of the layers means you will only be packing 4 sets, which hardly takes up any space at all. You will also notice that I haven't listed any bed wear such as pyjamas, that's correct, as you can use your base layer for sleeping in. You want to pack as little as possible and this is one trick to do so. Your base layers will do the job perfectly for sleeping in.

Once you run out of layers you can always try turning them in and out a few times, try and push what you have till laundry day. You might have to juggle them around, but you can always find a couple of sets clean enough to get you through a few more days. I always joke with my family that I wear my underwear 4 times before I wash them, turn them inside out and then flip them around. I'm only joking but I have been known to do this a rare few times. Do push your clothes as much as possible till laundry day. Stop being so self-conscious and live a little! You're travelling, who cares if you smell?

There is no need to go and buy expensive special technical clothing for the base layers; you can just take what you have in your wardrobe. You don't have to waste money, as tempting as it might be, what you're wearing is doing a good job, so why not use it. If it breaks or rips you can always buy a new one on the road or repair it with a compact sewing kit. I've seen T-shirts for £50 that are light weight, quick dry and a list of other things. They are great, don't get me wrong, but I want to get you travelling not wasting money on things you might need. If you want to invest later this is up to you, but at this point what you have works, so use it.

To make the baselayers items more compact, you might consider using ankle socks; this cuts the socks into half the size. With t-shirts you can have the option of wearing tank tops for hotter climates, and with underwear, these can be Y-fronts or thongs to cut the size even further down in your bag. For girls you might consider those all in one chuck over dresses or possibly a sarong. If you want to go even lighter then the options are there.

Over layers

1 x Swim Shorts

1 x Light Shorts

1 x Light Trousers

1 x Light Jeans

1 x Fleece or Hoodie

1 x Shirt

1 x Belt

You'll be changing your base layers everyday, which means your over-layers will remain clean enough to be washed once a week. When packing light you don't want to take extra; one jumper is better than taking six. It's just extra bulk which won't be used as often, your backpack is not a wardrobe you will need to make sacrifices when packing. It may sound crazy at first but using what you have to the max is the key to packing light.

Swim wear is a personal choice, be it a bikini set or bathers it's up to you. For guys the lightest option you can pack will be Speedo's. They take up no space at all, although they might not be the most stylish option. The beaches of Australia might be more suited to board shorts, which are great as they will double up as shorts. Personally I find they don't have enough pockets, but my swim shorts do come in handy for laundry day as you can wear these whilst you wash your other items. Another benefit of board shorts is they only take a couple of hours to dry and you can wash them in a sink.

Next on the list is a pair of light shorts, make sure they are not too bulky as they can take forever to dry out. They come in handy whilst visiting hot destinations when jeans just don't work. I like to get a pair with lots of pockets to store my passport, wallet, and keys in.

Light trekker trousers with detachable zip off shorts

Double up as shorts when you need another pair and pack very light, if you don't have them then you can always pack a light pair of trousers, especially if you have opted for Swim shorts. Some situations are not best for jeans, such as walking long distance, so trek trousers/light trousers help in these situations. When I'm just travelling to cities, I tend to not bring this item as I hardly use them, but again this is down to what you plan on doing. I'm 50/50 on this item myself, but they do come in handy in some situations when jeans don't work.

Jeans

Jeans just work, So many travellers say they are a nightmare to travel with but I think they are wrong. Yes they are hard to dry when wet but you put them to good use and look more normal when walking around urban surroundings. You can use them to go clubbing, perfect for long flights and comfortable for many occasions. An advantage of jeans is you can wear them for extremely long periods of times without having to wash them. You can practically live in them.

Shirt

Optional item, but perfect for when you want to dress and impress in a night club. Many travellers actually swap the 5 x t-shirts for shirts - it comes down to preference at the end of the day. I think it's smart to take at least one when you're visiting tricky borders or embassies in order to avoid looking like a hippy, which could cause problems. There will be times on your trip when you want to let your hair down and escape the backpacker scruffy look for a night. When you bring a shirt, it's perfect for these moments, along with a pair of jeans.

Fleece

Teamed up with your rain jacket, you will have yourself a very warm team. It's important that just like your jacket; you invest in something that's going to work for the duration of your trip. I like to use a micro fleece as they are light, warm, and breathable. It also doesn't need to be washed as much and they tend to dry very quickly. Normally it only takes 30 minutes out of the washing machine to be ready to wear and they're very warm under rain jackets.

Hooded jumper

I take both a fleece and a hooded jumper, you realistically only need one. I like to take both just in case one gets wet. The other can keep you warm whilst it dries. Hooded jumpers are bulky but they're great for sleeping on flights and looking cool. I have a light weight North Face quick dry hooded jumper that works really well. It is extra space, but I wear the hooded jumper every day and use the fleece as back up.

Belt

Keeps everything up, rather than down. For extra awesomeness you can find belts with built-in bottle openers, this comes in very handy for parties. For a party trick you can joke that you can open up bottles with your belly button; works every time.

Now you're fully clothed, by following all the above tips your bag should be looking pretty empty. Don't be alarmed that it's too little, you learn to adapt as you go along. If you're unsure with your gear you can always do a practice trip to the next city from your town or go and visit a family member who lives close and try out all your gear. Then at least it's easy to return home and rethink your strategy. This might be a good option if you're a worried type, as it saves packing hours before your big flight in a panic. If you have already done a practice drill a week before and you're satisfied, then it gives some reassurance before your trip.

Lugging unnecessary things around the world is just a pure pain, the above is the bare minimum you need in order to travel long term. It's better to take less and visit the laundry every 7-10 days along the way. Play around with the suggestions and choose what best suits your personal preference.

Cold Climates

The way to work around the weather is to avoid countries during their coldest season. For example, during winter in the UK it's summer in Australia, juggle these climates and you'll be fine. Yes, even Finland has some sun during parts of the year if you can believe it!

When you can't avoid the season or you love cold places (I am one of them), there is an additional winter kit list which can be added onto the above list.

As follows:

1 x Thermal Hat

1 x Insulated Gloves

1 x Thermal Top

1 x Long Johns

1 x Buff Headset

You can pack the items into the hat and then it doesn't take up a lot of space in your bag. When layered along with the original kit list it will add an extra addition of warmth. It's all about layers to keep warm, not bulk! That's the secret and it works with cold temperatures of up to -10C.

Bearing in mind, I have past experiences with sub zero conditions. If you have never experienced cold temperatures in your life, then you might want to purchase some warmer clothes when you arrive. If you have never experienced the cold then you might be from such locations as Brazil or Hawaii where it doesn't exist. This isn't a problem and the above solution might not work for you, but one tip would be not to buy cold weather gear in your home country. It can be very expensive if it is not commonly found. A solution would be to buy it when you arrive in the cold country which will be fully stocked and more affordable.

This is an important tip as warm clothing will be expensive where you live but the destination that is cold will of course be fully supplied with warm gear at more competitive prices.

Wonderful! You're clothed and ready to go! But of course there are still some important pieces of kit you need to bring as well.

Chapter Ten: Hygiene

Wash kit

It's very important to keep yourself clean and ready for another day, let this slip and you can become ill very quickly. Plus its ok to be smelly backpacker, but people around you might not agree with this (specially if your on a long haul flight). Here is what I pack in my wash kit:

1 x Airport friendly clear zip lock bag

1 x Waterproof string bag

1 x Toothbrush

1 x Toothpaste

1 x Dental floss

1 x Re-usable soap bottle

1 x Wet wipes

1 x Roller ball deodorant

1 x Electric razor

1 x Ear plugs in travel case

2 x Condoms in travel case

1 x Nail clip

1 x Cotton ear buds

A waterproof string bag is great and it's one of the pieces of kit I've had the longest. Avoid bulky oversized wash bags which take up too much space. A simple waterproof drawstring bag (500ml capacity) is very compact and fits all the above items in easily. You can secure the top with a knot by using the string so if anything breaks in your wash bag, it doesn't leak all over the rest of your bag.

Airports are still tight on liquid items, which means it's best to be prepared. You're going to be taking hand luggage so everything has to be under 100ml and stored in a clear zip lock bag. I put all my items in this bag, then into the string bag. I never take the zip lock bag out of the string bag, just the string bag and it scans perfectly fine through security. Normally I store this at the top of my bag for quick access at airports. Saves a lot of time and hassle and then you can whizz through the airport.

Dental hygiene

I tend to get the toothpaste with the built in mouth wash to save space, normally I buy the travel edition size and fill it up with bigger tubes when they run out, to save money. I think my travel size tube has 12 different types of toothpaste in it at the moment, but it's cheap to do as the travel editions are very expensive for what they are. For dental floss I use toothpicks with floss on the end (looks like a horseshoe shape), they are small and can be connected to the cotton ear buds, to keep them organized.

Reusable soap bottle

With an empty 100ml clear bottle, I don't think I've purchased soap in a very long time. Lots of places give free soap away in the toilets, hotels, airplanes and even some hostels. So when you have access to some, put it in your bottle. This way you never have to pay for soap, which adds up to a lot if you have a shower every day.

Nail clippers

Taking hand luggage will mean you can't pack your trusty Swiss army knife. One of the two most important items I use on mine is the bottle opener (Which should now be built into your belt), nail Scissors and the file. Buying a compact nail clipper and file set will mean you can check it onto your flight. It's also a very important item for another reason. If you don't cut your toe nails it can cause problems for your feet when walking long distances. It causes pain and friction when constantly walking which will happen a lot on your trip. Keep your nails trimmed and avoid this from happening. Also your finger nails can collect a lot of dirt, best to keep on top of your hygiene and avoid becoming ill.

Earplugs

Handy for hostels when they're located too close to a main street, or when you are sleeping too close to a fellow roommate who likes to trumpet throughout the night. If you have a friend who is a builder, ask nicely if you can grab a pair for free. Normally they have them sitting around and can easily grab a pair, rather than forking out a lot at the airport or travel store.

Condoms

Even females should pack them too. I know it can be embarrassing, but be an adult about it. You can even buy compact travel cases to keep them in, so when you're going through an airport with your toiletries they are discreetly stored. Travel with condoms, it's smart.

Electric Razor

For the hairy men out there (and of course girls as well), I also pack an electric beard trimmer with a European adapter which seems to work everywhere. I just use it for beard trimming once a week when I'm doing the laundry and it works wonders. This saves having to buy razors and soap all the time. You can get ones for standard shaving as well depends how often you have to shave, as one razor a month might work out for you. For me on the other hand I need to shave twice a day for a clean shave so the beard trimmer works universally and does the trick for me.

Chapter Eleven: Technology

The most useful tools you can pack will be technology. It will keep you connected with the outside world and everyone back home. You will be able to save a lot of money by buying and researching your next destination online, and most importantly, it will keep you entertained on those long journeys.

You may be wondering why you want to bring technology on your trip; after all, don't you want to get away from it all? You don't have to pack it if that's the adventure you're after, but bringing it along will keep you organized and save you a lot of money.

Smart Phone

Smart phones are focused on quickly grabbing all the information you want in a minimalistic environment. Personally, I think they are the tool that all travellers should have. You won't waste a lot of time online and you'll be able to do all the fun things travelling brings. You're not going on holiday with the internet; you're using the internet to make your travel more enjoyable. You're enjoying the values of the offline world with the support of the online world. It will take some time to get into the swing of things, but over time you will wonder how on earth you ended up wasting so much time on the internet. If someone really wants to contact you, they will contact you in a quick enough way that you find out soon enough. So let your online world stay at home and use a smart phone for minimal web use so you can focus on what you really have set out to do; travel.

To do all the things you want to do on your travels; your smart phone will take care of the digital side of things. You can edit and upload photos straight from the phone these days as well as upload blog posts and do online banking. The list is endless. Here is just a small list of what you can do with a Smart phone:

• Make phone calls (www.skype.com Discount/free worldwide calls)

• Send text messages

• Tell the time (in all time zones)

• Email

• PDF reader for E-Tickets and Books ECT

• MP3 player

• Radio

• Alarm clock

• Video recorder

• Voice recorder

• Internet browser

• Watch videos

• Online banking

• Camera

- Air mile reward apps

- Flight trackers

- Hostel booking apps

You get the idea, plus much, much more. All the items you would have used in the past to do some of the above have now been replaced by this device. It's allowing you to travel more compact and lighter.

All this incredible power in your pocket! If you explained to someone in the 80's what a smartphone could do they would probably call you crazy. In fact the whole space mission to the moon was completed with less memory than what a smartphone has today. We are lucky to have such devices, and it's a shame it's often taken for granted.

My Choice?

Apple iPhone 5s

Laptop

Working whilst you're travelling? You will need a laptop, simple. You can try to work on a smart phone but you're going to have a tough time as it's hard to work long hours on a smart phone.

There are lots of wonderful laptops that are suited for light weight travel such as Ultra-books. If you plan on running a business online whilst you travel, this might be the best option for you. My laptop of choice is the Apple MacBook Air 11inch. It's the laptop choice of many digital nomads and can work for you. I choose the MacBook Air because it's built to be light, but also strong in order to withstand the elements. It's also extremely thin, light and operates just as well as any powerful desktop computer. It can do a lot of the things you would expect a powerful computer to do. In fact I'm writing this book on it right now in The Netherlands; works like a dream. Pay a little extra and invest in an Ultra-book rather than a cheap Netbook which are a little outdated now by tablets. It's best to shop around online for Ultra-books and see what suits you best.

Amazon Kindle

The Amazon Kindle is a device which allows you to read digital books on the move. It uses an E-ink technology which consumes a low amount of energy and is very easy on the eyes to read, almost like a real book itself. The Amazon Kindle has completely changed the way I travel and consume books. If you want to pack minimally, ideally you would not take a Kindle as you can read books on your smart phone. But there are lots of advantages to packing a Kindle, such as the battery life which is outstanding. Because of its low level of technology it's pretty much used in the same way as a calculator. Because of this, fully charged it can last up to a couple of months.

If you were to read a book on a laptop or smart phone, it will drain your battery very quickly. That's why the Amazon Kindle is perfect for long distance journeys, as it takes a long time for the battery to drain. This means you can be entertained by lots of books for days on end. Also, packing guidebooks can take up a lot of space and almost weigh as much as an elephant which is horrible for your back as well as the space in your bag. It's very light weight and compact, which is perfect for travelling. Plus a lot of the major guidebooks are available to purchase on the Kindle. Another good point is you can download lots of free books, as well as paid books which are priced very competitively. Comparing the prices that bookshops charge for English versions abroad, you can save a lot of money with a Kindle.

Adapters and cables

The last thing you want to pack is a bundle of cables and travel adapters; they get all tangled up and can take up a lot of space. If you decide to purchase an Apple Mac and iPhone, you can purchase the Apple travel Adapter kit as it comes with all the international plugs which fit onto the Mac power cord (Mac safe). Did you know that you can charge your smart phone and Kindle off the USB port of the Mac? This means with a Mac safe and the international adapter kit you can charge your other devices off the Mac saving you having to travel with loads of power converter and plugs for all your devices. This is the best solution I've come across that's worked very well. This solution is very minimal and hardly takes up any space in your bag. You can even buy a 2 x USB charging head that fits onto your Mac safe and comes with the international adapters, so this can work out to be an even better solution for charging your other devices.

Headphones

Don't waste a lot of money on expensive headphones, you simply don't need them. In fact you can become a target by wearing them, keep a low profile and stick to an inexpensive pair. If you can't wear ear buds and want to purchase a headset with great sound but don't want to spend a lot of money, I recommend Koss Portable headset, which is very affordable and great for travelling. They fold up and curl into themselves to become very compact and easy to travel with. I use them a lot because of the good quality. But if you can get on with ear buds, they are the most compact and best to travel with. You can buy ear buds with a built in microphone for sound recording or for use with applications like Skype to give you some privacy.

All of the above products that I have recommended in this section can be found on my website. You can find all the items in my gear section and can even purchase them directly from the links. If you want, you can actually purchase my whole bag with one click and have it all delivered by the next day. This is more for the crazy trustworthy reader, but it's all very possible from www.traveldave.co.uk. Also in the video section of my site, you can find packing tips on how to pack and prepare your bag for your next adventure. As well as a more in depth review of all of the above products and how to best use them.

Chapter Twelve: Optional Items

Extra items which you can also choose to pack.

Sewing Kit

I've used it time to time for buttons or rips, as it can save you some money and you can find smaller ones for free in Christmas crackers so keep a look out for them. I have had these embarrassing moments where my shorts have just split. It's not a great situation to be in, but popping along to a restroom and taking out your sewing kit can save you in such emergency situations. Then you can pop along on your journey without flashing your undies at everyone. Life-saving some might say.

Compact Towel

Some places you will stay will have a towel on offer, but not all places will. Some even charge which adds up to a lot of money. Best to buy a micro towel, they don't cost a lot of money and in the long run it will return its investment. Don't bring a full sized towel, they are extremely bulky. This towel takes up very little space and comes in handy when you need it.

Water bottle

This will save you a lot of money. Most water found around the world is drinkable (check before you do!), and in most cases all you need is 1-2 litres. Buying bottled water is not only bad for the environment; it's bad for your wallet. I used a compact platypus 1 litre water bottle that rolls up and fits compactly in my bag side pocket. It also has a clip so it doesn't fall out of my bag and I can secure it to a strap. Because it folds up I'm able to take it onto flights when it's empty and fill it up on the other side when we've landed. Water bottle's really work magic whilst travelling, and save a lot of money in expensive tourist destinations.

There really is no need to buy bottled water. Even in locations where it's not safe to drink, they will normally offer some sort of filtered water cooler system for guests.

Compact silk sheet

Expensive, but totally worth it. A one person silk sheet will fit into the palm of your hand. It's simply a single sheet to keep you comfortable and warm while you sleep, but yet not as bulky as a sleeping bag. It's also very hostel friendly as it can be washed easily and not attract bed bugs, which is what hostels hate about sleeping bags. Not all hostels, but some charge for sheets so you can save money having a silk liner. They are also handy for long bus rides or airports when you want to have a quick snooze. Why silk and not cotton? It's much warmer and a lot lighter, so it will save you space in your bag for extra things.

Notebook and Pen

You can be paperless and use a smart phone to jot down notes, but sometimes you can't beat a good old notebook and pen. Great for taking to coffee shops and writing down the next big idea, jotting down the next hostel's address, writing down that cute girl's email address or simply drawing a picture of an apple to help you get by in a Japanese supermarket. You don't need it, but some people can't live without it (like me!). My notebook of choice is a Moleskine as they are leather bound and built for travellers. Ernest Hemingway himself used to use these, so worth checking out and you might become an addict just like me.

Padlock with secure number feature

In some hostels you might have to use your own lock on your locker, best to bring one along so you can save some money on those occasions. You can also get a lock for your laptop for extra security in your hostel, or when you're working at a coffee shop so no one can grab and run off with it when you go for a second cup. purchasing a numbered lock will help having to worry about keys, just make sure its a number your remember and wont be easy for people to figure out themselves (not 1,2,3,4,5,6 Please!).

Sunglasses

It's going to be sunny on your travels so make sure you pack your shades. One tip; make sure they are protected from UV light so you don't damage your eyes. It's up to you if you want to buy designer or cheap disposable ones on the beach. I like to buy things that are built to last so I go for an average non branded pair and they seem to last well. Cheap beach ones seem to only last a few days and that's not very good for the environment.

Chapter Thirteen: The Art of Packing Light

The aim of the game is to be able to pack in a flash. The last thing you want to do on your travels is spend hours packing every time you change location. This is going to happen a lot so you want to create a system that works for you to make packing quick and easy. I have already gone through the list of the bare minimum you should pack; now we should create a system.

Your bag:

Your bag is your new home, and just like a home you have many rooms. You should look at your bag in the same way as a house. Divide your bag mentally in your head and then plan which item should go where. Now this is going to be tricky, but working out a system that works will help you in the long run.

Some items will fit better in one place rather than another; this is what you have to work out. Round items shouldn't be placed at the bottom of your bag; you want to place flat items to make use of the dynamics of the bag. This will allow you to make full use of the size of the bag which is limited due to hand luggage restrictions. This is why it's important that nothing goes to waste and areas of the bag remain empty.

Another packing tip is to ensure that heavy items are centralized in the bag and not at the bottom, top or outside to ensure equal weight distribution. This will make your bag feel lighter and will allow yourself to be more comfortable when it's full. If you pack a heavy item in these locations it could offset the bag and cause you back ache which is never a good thing.

Use the sections in your bag in the way they have been designed. What I mean by this is; if there is a pen slot then your pen will ideally fit there. I Know it's pretty much common sense but you should use all parts of these bags to work out what item fits well where. You will have to experiment with this as some items will fit better in another place.

- Passport in passport pocket
- Pen in pen holder
- Sunglasses in top flap that's sunglasses shape,
- Kindle in book shaped area
- Wires in mesh pocket.
- Wash kit on top for easy grab
- Clothes in central section
- Flip flops in the flat front section of the bag
- Water bottle in water bottle pocket

You get the idea. Bag designers understand what you might be packing and have designed the bag in a certain way, so work out which bit of the kit fits where. This will allow you to maximize the space you have as it's very limited.

Air is your enemy

What If I told you a lot of the space that's taken up in your bag is actually just air? Fold your jumper and then push your hand down on it. It's not reacting in the same way a solid laptop would, it will move, so why are you packing air? It's pretty much going to be present in all of your clothes. My tip? Purchase a 1 litre nylon water proof air tight bag. All of the base layers will fit perfectly in this, possibly even the shorts as well. What you want to do is stuff it all in, sit on it (get all that air out) then roll and lock. Instantly you will notice how a lot of things have turned into a handful of things and will now fit in a more snug way in your bag. This is also a system which allows you to quickly pack and be on your way.

Waist and chest straps

Bottom line; use them whenever possible and especially when on long journeys. They are on the bag for a reason and that's to help support the load in equal weight around the body. The waist straps are designed for your hips to take the load. It should be doing such a good job that no weight is put on your shoulders, and so well that you can put your hand between the shoulder straps and your shoulders. Your hips can take it and that's what the waist strap is for. The chest strap (if your bag has one) helps your shoulder straps from spreading apart and will keep a central location along your chest. This stops your bag from wobbling and allows your waist strap to do its job. There you go, now you know what they are really for.

Bag up loose sections

Hopefully you will find the perfect places for your items around your bag. To make it even easier to pack, you might want to group up items into small string bags to make it easier to organize. This will help you stuff many items at once into your bag and then when you need them quickly go to the small bag you need. Just keeps everything together. Just like what you've done with some of your clothes and wash kit already. An example could be a bag for your wires and plugs. This will just speed up the whole packing process.

Now, when the time comes, and you've forgotten to set your alarm clock the previous night and you have 3 hours to get to the airport, you will be ready and prepared like a travelling ninja to pack all your stuff in no time!

Now it's all in line, there is one last step you should do with your gear.

Document your items

do as follows:

• What it is, brand type, colour, cost, spec, and so on (write it down on a spreadsheet).

• Take pictures of all your items, one together and then one in sections (tech, clothes, and toiletries.)

• Take pictures of all the receipts or scan them if you can or keep the digital copy if you have got one.

• Write down all the serial numbers or codes for all of your valuables as well as Brand names and model types.

Then finally when you have done all of the above attach it all in an email and send it to yourself as well as a parent (with their permission), with the subject line: **In case of an emergency**. You can also send it to a trusted friend or next of kin/other family member that you trust.

You might as well attach a copy of your passport as well and a copy of important documents such as insurance forms, a small list of 10 close contacts you might need (address, email, phone number).

If you have a www.Dropbox.com account, Google drive or Evernote account you might want to upload it all here as well. Another option is to purchase a small USB stick to keep on you at all times. But taking all the above steps will give you a lot of options to access this information if needed.

keep a few photocopies of your passport in your wallet and bag in case your passport gets stolen, you will have a copy of your main ID then. Also pack 10 passport style photos in your wallet which will come in handy when you have to apply for visa's on the road.

Doing the following will really help you out if you're in an emergency situation such as needing to access your contacts or if you want to claim on your insurance for your items if your bag gets stolen.

Being prepared in such a way will really help you out if you need to make a claim.

This packing section has formed the basis of how you will pack for the rest of your life. That's why it's so important to get it right first time and then learn and build off that process. You will be ready to jump into any adventure and you can stick to this kit list for a long time. Next time you have to go somewhere you can easily pack and go and be ready for where ever the next step will take you.

Chapter Fourteen: Transportation

This section is all about hacking transportation to make it more accessible by juggling between the different methods or sorting out the best deal for the right journey. Being a little smarter in this area can save you a lot of time and money.

When it comes to travelling, today's generation is extremely lucky. What once was a long 5 day journey from London to New York City by boat; is now a simple 7 hour flight.

Transportation has never been so affordable and so frequently available as transport networks keep getting bigger and wider. Many journeys that were once a lifetime event are now everyday commutes for some people.

Chapter fifteen: Booking Flights Like A Travel Ninja

There are hundreds of airlines all competing to get your credit card details and putting your bum onto their seats. It's very common for a bundle of airlines to fly the exact same route. Armed with some travel hacking skills you can unlock the secrets of how to take advantage of these rock bottom prices.

Flights will be the biggest area of spending when taking time out to travel. If you focus your energy here it will be time well spent. The more you save on the flights the more you can travel. Getting this right can be the difference between a short trip and a long one.

Here I'm going to reveal all of my travel booking secrets. When it comes to booking flights over the years I've created a system that both works and has saved me lots of money in the process. It's no longer just a simple act; it's a whole operation that I take very seriously. In some ways I think of it as an art form as it's been many years in the making in order to get the process just right and to work universally for all airlines. With a little time and patience, you too can book flights like a pro. Here is my method to finding cheap flights and how you too can adapt to using this process.

First step; sign up to all the major airlines and budget airline's emailing list.

"I hate spam" you scream! Do you want to find a cheap flight before everyone else? Then sign up to their email list.

One major reason why I've been able to grab affordable flights has been because I found out by email before everyone else. This limited window of time can be the difference between bagging a cheap flight or not.

Airlines like repeat customers and love to reward them in as many ways as they can, after all, they are nothing without their customers. People who are signed up for their emailing list are considered as repeat customers, because you normally subscribe when booking a flight. This is the main reason why airlines first tell their email list about crazy sale deals well before anyone else.

It has a ripple effect. Mostly people on their mailing list have travelled with them before and are happy to do so again. Repeat customers are easy to invite back again, it's free advertisement for the airline as after they have booked they will talk about it with their friends face to face or use social media and everyone else will find out about it.

 Because they have flown with them they already know what the experience is like and are happy to promote the products they have enjoyed. This is normally the time when everyone else finds out about the flight sale and then it's too late as all the good deals are already taken. A lot of people at this point have worked themselves up so much about travelling they will book it anyway. This is why airlines have sales and this is why you should learn why the airlines do it. Think like an airline and you will be able to get the deals that they offer as promotional tools.

Sign up for the mailing list and be one step ahead of the rest. Take budget airlines for example that avoid paying for advertising as much as possible in order to pass the price on to you. A mailing list is an affordable method of advertisement for budget airlines to use as it doesn't cost them a lot of money to set up and run. You will be the first to know, so sign-up and get ready for those deals to come along.

Waiting by your Inbox

Normally airlines will only do silly deals twice a year; when their sales are slow or when the airline is just getting desperate. When this time comes, be prepared to jump as they won't be around for much longer. Also look out for airlines having a system glitch, normally a human era on the system that posts a flight at a silly price. This happens time to time and in most cases only a few people book so the airline honours the flights on goodwill as it was their mistake.

One place to look out for such deals is: www.Holidaypirates.com

I know it's a pain to keep a lot of airlines on your mailing list, but the amount of money you will be saving will totally be worth it. If it really bugs you, and your email account is your pride and joy, then you can always set up a different email account just for receiving flight deals. Just make sure you check it frequently to get the benefits.

One example, Air New Zealand:

www.airnewzealand.co.nz/email-offer-signup

Facebook and Twitter

The new advertisement portal, many airlines are now buckling onto the trend of social media and using Facebook/Twitter to promote their latest deals. You might prefer to follow them on these channels instead to find out all the latest sale promotions, this method is growing in popularity.

I've saved a lot of money by waiting for sales, as many airlines repeat the same ones every year. Booking around the sale season for summer/winter flights (January/February or April/May) is a good idea as they don't normally get that low any other time of the year, Specially want to avoid the peek times (November/December or July/August).

One Example, AirAsia

Facebook: www.facebook.com/AirAsia

Twitter: www.twitter.com/AirAsia

Let the flight come to you

The most expensive flight you will ever pay for will be emergency flights. It's no longer the case that airlines use last minute deals. That's simply an old system that doesn't work anymore. For example, a few years ago being on standby for a flight and jumping on if there was a free seat used to be possible at a knock down price. Now airlines see those seats as last minute gold for people who urgently need to get to a location and will pay whatever it costs. This is just a shift in the market place as flying becomes something we are all used to like a bus service, it's no longer a luxury reserved for a few.

The airline will have you in their hands and you will have to pay whatever they ask for. This is not a nice situation to be in and it's better to be the other way around. Take what the airline can't sell and grab it at a rock bottom price. This won't work out every time but if you don't care where you're going and just want to travel; this can be a fun method of travelling. I've ended up in some fun random places following this method and sometimes I had no intention of going, but some deals are too good to be missed.

The aim is not to be picky and to go with whatever is on offer.

When you have found an airline that's having a sale, here are some simple steps to take in order to find those cheap flights:

Break down the email's terms and conditions.

Once you have received an email about a sale which interests you, the next step is to break down what's on offer. Now you need to read the small print and work it out from there. Here is what you need to look for in the small print:

- Destination airport
- Black out period (Public holidays, sporting events, etc.)
- Date of booking
- Date of flying

- Indication of times you might have to fly between

This is a good time to also work out if the airport is close to the location that you intend to travel to. Some airports can be hours from the city centre and you need to consider this cost into your final price. What might look like a deal, might not be.

How to layout the dates you have gathered from the sales terms and conditions:

Its all going to look like a very confusing puzzle game, to help you better understand the dates your playing with its best to use a calendar to map it all out. Before you go out running to the supermarket to buy a calendar if you have a printer at hand it can be more simple.

Windows users: Outlook

Apple users: ICal

Linux or any for that matter: www.google.com/calendar

Using the above you can print out blank months of the year to help you with booking your sale flight. Simple print out the months that the sale flights are available.

Now you can fill out the details onto the calendar of the dates that you can fly. This may be the destination, date on offer or the time you have to fly between. This will make the search for the cheapest flights easier as the terms and conditions are normally indications of where the sale prices can be.

But before you move on make sure you scribble out the blackout periods, these are dates that the airline cannot honour with the sale, possibly related to a major sporting event or public holiday in that city and pretty much all the seats have already been allocated.

What you should be looking at is a calendar with blacked out boxes and dates filled out were sale prices might possibly be found. Now you can start placing your pieces to the puzzle to see the bigger picture.

Next step you want to go to the airline search engine. It's normally best at this point to start listing destinations mentioned in the promotion that are most important to you. Pick what places you want to go to the most out of what is on offer. Then you can work your way down the list until you find something that's matched. You can also black out personal dates that you can't attend due to exams or birthdays ECT. Make sure the flight works out for you; that's the most important thing.

Now you will be armed with the most useful Calendar to help you find those cheap flights on the airline's search engine. You will not be a headless chicken looking in the wrong areas for the sale price.

All you're doing now is matching the calendar with the system search engine and through trial and era, discover the sale price. Most airline search engines will allow you to compare and look at flights, weeks at a time. This is perfect as you click next to unveil the next week's prices; this allows searching to be quick and painless. This way you can spot sale prices a lot quicker.

The worst airlines will only give you the date searched for which means it will take some time, but hang in there! These come with the best rewards as people give up quickly on these ones. You might have a better chance compared to the more faster to skim through search engines.

Keep repeating this process for different destinations until you get a bite. Bingo! Once you've found it you can bag it, go to the check-out and you're away. I've used this method a lot and as a word of warning; it can get clogged because of the busy traffic but keep at it, the flights are there waiting to be discovered. It can be time consuming putting all the data entries in, but you soon get used to it.

Normally the cheap unbelievable flights are impossible to find, but it is there if you can act fast, I guarantee it. If it's not there then it's either been taken by some other lucky person who got there first, or its false advertisement. An airline can get into trouble for false advertisement, so its 100% there or they are breaking the law.

The best way to look at this searching method is to turn it into a game. I always compare it to digital fishing, it takes a lot of searching but when you get a bite it's yours till the credit card transaction goes through. Some people might think this is sad, but you can really be well in front of the rest by using this method and you won't be laughing when you're relaxing on the beaches of Thailand at no cost at all.

How to find cheap flights away from the sales

If you're set on a particular destination and want to find an affordable flight away from the sales, there are still some useful tips to follow to find an affordable flight.

Avoid busy week days such as fly Friday, return Sunday. Choose to fly on alternative days such as Thursday or Saturday, and return Monday. Choose to also fly at odd times such as 6am or 11pm where the majority of cheaper flights will be found. Fly to the not so popular airport locations such as London Stansted or Frankfurt Hahn which are always cheaper than the major city airports and can still be reached by bus at an affordable price. Book your flight around two to three months in advance, any earlier and the flight will be at a block price, anytime closer to the flight the price will be a premium. Normally two to three months is the perfect time frame to book a flight at its most affordable. Also avoid booking during busy periods such as public holidays or sporting events, aim to book when it's a little quieter during the season. See if flying into an alternative city might be cheaper. For example, Bratislava is a cheap short train ride away from Vienna and is easily connected.

Pay with a credit card when possible

If the airline goes under and files for bankruptcy, your flight goes with them as does all the flights. This puts you in a horrible situation and you might never see your flight or money back ever again, unless you have very good insurance that covers these situations. However, if you book with a credit card, you gain an amount of protection where you can phone the credit card company and tell them that the flight never took off. Legally it's a failed transaction as they haven't delivered the service they charged you for, so the credit card company can cancel your flight and return the money. Just a useful protection trick I picked up along the way which can help you in those horrible situations.

Stopovers

The most expensive flights will be direct but many airlines are happy to undercut direct flights with stop offs along the way to connect with their other aircrafts/alliance partners. This can save you a lot of money for a few extra hours on top of your flight time. Just make sure that the airport you're stopping off at will allow you to be a transit passenger without a visa as this could cause some problems with immigration. The majority of the time it can really work out. Take Iceland Air (www.icelandair.co.uk) for example, who fly from London to New York via

Reykjavik. You can also choose to stop off in Iceland's capital for a few days along the way at no additional cost and they are normally much more affordable compared to booking direct.

Flight search engine

www.kayak.com

www.momondo.com

www.hipmunk.com

The above three websites are flight search engines. I use them all individually and like them for different reasons. It's good to use three, as you get a variety of results in return and can judge if you have a deal or not. The downside to this is you can't search for budget airlines, as they tend to operate cheaper with direct sales.

Remember to always check on budget airlines websites directly because of this, search engines might not be the cheapest result but they will give you an idea of the price.

If you plan on flying from A to B and don't fancy waiting around for a sale to come along then place the destinations and dates into each search engine and hunt around to see what you can find. Its a good idea to see if it is possible to fly to the location your going to for cheap and which airline would be the cheapest. Using a number of search engines will allow you to compare the price and see if you have a deal or not. Juggling with the dates and alternative destinations can help to bring this price down and discover what works best.

Then you will want to go to the cheapest airline directly and input your results from the search engine to see if they are really the cheapest, you might find that it would be cheaper to book direct with that airline.

Using alternative airlines websites in different languages or currencies is also a good idea.

using Google Chrome with language translation and XE.com its now possible to compare the prices in different currencies and languages. This is due to some currencies being weaker than others and many promotions can be region specific. As funny as it sounds I've managed to find some very shocking differences in the past. For example, on Air Italia's Italian website I bagged a return flight, Rome to Beijing, for only £252. Shocking the booking went through, So it's worth checking these alternatives as a last resort, you never know what you might find.

Another tip, search in incognito mode (possible in Google Chrome browser). Search engines track your unique IP address and can notice when your searching for the same flight again and again. With this information they are able to rise the price every time you search. incognito stops this as your IP address is covered up.

Chapter Sixteen: Around the World Tickets (RTW)

The tool of the backpacker: The RTW ticket. This option when used correctly can be a real money saver. Rather than buying a simple return flight with a stopover at a fixed price, RTW tickets can be done in the same manner but allow you to stop off at the stopovers and extend the amount of time you want to visit in that area. Why spend 10 hours on a layover wasting away in the airport when you can jump off the flight for practically the same price and travel onwards a few months later once you've explored the place.

Here is the breakdown, normal flight and price:

£999 - Return flight London to Melbourne (with 7 hour stopover in Singapore there and back)

How RTW tickets work:

£999 - London - Singapore - Melbourne - Auckland - Los Angeles - New York - London

Here is what you can do with the above RTW flight when spaced out over a year:

Fly London to Singapore and stop off to explore South East Asia for 4 months with sleeper buses before returning back to Singapore. Then onto the next stop Melbourne and travel upwards along the Gold Coast from Sydney then return to Melbourne after 4 months. From here, fly over to New Zealand and explore the north and south island before returning to Auckland after 2 months. Then head over to LA and drive the coastal roads of California for a month before flying over to New York City and grabbing a bus to Boston and then onwards to Canada to see the Niagara Falls. From here you can go to Toronto, Montreal, Quebec city, Halifax before returning to New York to fly home to London.

As you can see, both flights cost the same amount. One is spread out over the space of 1 year and it would cost you the same as a simple return flight from London to Australia. With a RTW ticket you're unlocking a very affordable method of using air transportation. A Round the World ticket can unlock adventures and endless possibilities at an affordable price.

Little advice: Make sure you plan your RTW ticket with the seasons, the last thing you want to do is arrive in Australia during the winter; the beaches won't be a very enjoyable experience (it does get cold in Australia, which might come as a bit of a shock!).

As you can tell RTW tickets work the same as normal flights but they break up the connections to allow you to spend more time in said locations. This works by working with the airline alliances and allows them to free up seats that they can sell at a higher price to the one-way passengers. Flying doesn't have to be expensive when you play around with the system. It's simply applying the same amount of air miles for both flights and spreading them out amongst different destinations.

You can book RTW tickets at a number of travel agents or directly from RTW websites such as:

www.roundtheworldexperts.co.uk

With the travel agent:

www.statravel.co.uk/round-the-world-travel

Or directly from the airline alliance such as:

www.oneworld.com/flights/round-the-world-fares/oneworld-explorer/

Warning, don't get carried away! The above suggestion is a typical low cost RTW route, as it's using the most common major hubs that the alliances frequently use. It's very tempting to get carried away and fly to all the fun places you've always wanted to visit. The way you need to look at it is 10 or so different airlines fly from Singapore to Australia, this is not the case for routes such as Cambodia to Australia, it's far less frequent and will cost a lot more because of this. What you've quickly learned is convenience sells for a premium. Budget seekers however should have a lot of time and flexibility in order to grab cheap affordable flights. After all, that's why they are going cheap in the first place.

I've seen RTW tickets start around £599, but this is the very basic Australia return. The price will change depending on the Alliance/airline you go with and the time of year. Other things to take into consideration: the more exotic or hard to reach locations will cost you more. The more stop offs you make will cost you more and the dates/seasons will affect the final price. Stop-offs themselves should be limited to 4-6 to make it affordable and only use the RTW flight major hubs. Avoid choosing 20 or so just because you want to go everywhere, there are much cheaper methods to get to the location you want to visit.

My tip is to use the large hubs as location bases on your RTW flight.

It's much cheaper to fly domestically once you're in the continent using budget airlines and local transportation such as trains and buses. Once you have reached one of the major hubs in the continent you're visiting, you can then reach all the other places you want to visit at a better rate. Here are some suggestions of major hubs located in continents that you can reach with a RTW ticket:

South East Asia.

Major hubs for RTW: Singapore, Hong Kong, Bangkok.

South East Asian countries to explore from these hubs: Vietnam, Malaysia, Laos, Thailand, Indonesia, Burma, Cambodia.

You can use:

AirAsia - www.airasia.com

Tiger airways - www.tigerairways.com

SCOOT airlines - www.tigerairways.com

Jetstar - www.jetstar.com

or even take the long distance affordable sleeper buses all around South East Asia.

Central American:

Major Hubs: Mexico City, San José

Travel: Local buses and coaches (chicken buses)
Flying cheap around Mexico:

InterJet - www.interjet.com

Destination: Costa Rica, Panama, Mexico, El Salvador, Guatemala, Belize, Honduras, Nicaragua.

North America

Major hubs for RTW: Mexico City, New York City, Los Angeles, Toronto, Vancouver, Atlanta

Budget airlines:

Westjet - www.westjet.com

Canadian Air Affairs - www.canadianaffair.com

Jetblue - www.jetblue.com

Alternatives:

Greyhound - www.greyhound.com

Megabus - www.megabus.com

Destinations: Canada, USA, Mexico

Europe.

Major Hubs for RTW: London, Frankfurt, Amsterdam, Paris, Rome

Budget airlines:

Ryanair - www.ryanair.com

Easyjet - www.easyjet.com

Wizzair - www.wizzair.com

Air Berlin - www.airberlin.com

Alternatives:

Eurostar - www.eurostar.com

InterRail Pass - www.interrail.eu

Euroline - www.eurolines.com

Destinations: Nordics, Central Europe, Eastern Europe

I haven't listed all the areas around the world but you get the general idea from the above information. Once you use your affordable RTW ticket to get to one of the major hubs you can extend the next flight from that destination to depart 2 months later and then come back to the RTW ticket once you've explored the said area using the more affordable travel alternatives. This will bring the price of your trip down dramatically.

Once you have booked your RTW ticket depending on who you decide to go with you will also gain some other extra advantages over booking the tickets individually. Such as receiving your own personal 24/7 booking agent when you buy your RTW ticket (check when buying to see if the company offers this service) to assist you every step of the way on your trip and to offer support when you need it. You could then change your flight dates if you want to get back home early or stay a little longer in your destination. This may cost a fee or come along free of charge with the service depending on what company you're going to travel with. But one thing is for sure; it will be cheaper changing the flight with them than it will be to book a whole new flight all together. This is great, as it offers you protection if you get caught in an emergency situation where you have to change your plans.

Chapter Seventeen: Flying Tips

Always travel economy

I once read a fantastic article about a once famous actor who is no longer successful and he was asked what his biggest mistake was in his life. He said travelling first class. Once you have had a taste of the good life you will want more. The best way to avoid this is to not do it at all. There is nothing wrong with travelling coach/economy, it gets you there from A to B and then you will be used to travelling this way. Once you have experienced travelling first class you will always want to travel first class. Help your mindset and never do it. Of course it's tempting if you get offered a discounted upgrade but stay strong and always focus towards travelling cheap and in economy.

Picking Your Seat

www.seatguru.com

A large majority of airlines will let you choose your seat in advance at no extra cost. Do it. It's going to cost you nothing and you can easily locate the best seat on the aircraft using the wonderful website, Seat Guru. There are lots of terrible seats on different types of aircrafts and you can avoid being assigned one by checking out a map of the aircraft in advance and spot the best seat. If it costs extra then don't worry it's not worth the cost, just skip it.

Take hand luggage and avoid extras

As explained in the 'packing' section, you're only going to be travelling with hand luggage. This means you're avoiding having to pay for those expensive check-in baggage fees. You really can just travel with hand luggage across continents, and I've done it many times. Once you get the sense of being free with hand luggage, you never look back and you save a packet.

If you have to pay to choose a seat don't bother, you're getting on the flight and they will give you a seat automatically. I've been asked by friends before if you don't select a seat, where will they put you? I can 100% guarantee that it will be in the plane, they can't strap you onto the wing! Avoid paying this extra crazy fee and put it towards a nice affordable beach hut in Indonesia. Tidy.

Priority boarding or speedy boarding? Don't bother, what a waste! Everyone is getting on the plane, why do you need to be the first? Many times I've made this point to those who have purchased such stupid services. What I do is wait for them to be asked up first, then wait for the normal passengers to board and walk faster than them to the door of the plane. It's a little bit cheeky, but it just goes to show how pointless this service is.

This can relate to many other fees such as credit card transaction costs, you're simply stuck in a situation where you have no choice but to pay it. However do try alternative methods of card types, as some cards might be free or cheaper to use. I really hate this fee as the airline is simply charging you to take your money, which seems stupid. Currently this transaction fee is under investigation in Europe and the situation has got a lot better recently.

Also make sure you check-in online and print out your boarding ticket before you head to the airport. Some airlines require you to do so or they will charge you a penalty fee and this could cost you a small fortune. Avoid this fee and print it off before you arrive. It's also very handy to do this as you're travelling with hand luggage and can head straight to security, saving you a lot of time at the airport.

Air miles

Did you know that if you fly to Australia and back from London, whilst collecting air miles you can pretty much get a free domestic flight within Europe? All you have to do to gain those air miles is sign up to the airline's program and then give them your membership card upon check in. Simple.

Because all of the above is going to take only a small amount of effort to do, it's totally worth it and won't take up any hassle at all, so why not? If you're going to fly with them you might as well collect them, they are there for the taking and will go to waste otherwise. In best cases its also free to sign up so it wont cost you a penny.

Just to quickly explain what an alliance is, its when airlines create a partnership between each other to expand routes and to increase customer levels. Air mile programs also partner up together so you don't loose out. this also means you can use lounges as well as many other services which are part of the same alliance. It's a win win for both the customer and the airline.

Little tip for collecting Air miles; just sign up to 3 airlines within the 3 main airline alliances and you will be pretty much all set for collecting Air miles. Once you're a member of one airline who is a member of the alliance, you can use the program to collect Air miles across all of them. This saves you a lot of time and saves you from carrying around a shed load of cards and gets you collecting quicker.

The 3 alliances are as follows (with the one airline I use as an example):

One World (British airways) www.oneworld.com

SkyTeam (KLM) www.skyteam.com

Star Alliance (Lufthansa) www.staralliance.com

These 3 alliances will pretty much cover the lot of them apart from those airlines that have their own program such as Virgin Atlantic's flying club (www.virgin-atlantic.com/en/gb/frequentflyer) for example. Keeping your Air miles within one airline will help you build them quicker and allow you to collect them from across other airline networks, it really works and you'll be stacking them up before you know it.

Other ways to earn Air miles

It's very possible to get flights completely free, yes, free! Many credit card companies have affiliate connections with the airline's Air mile schemes and offer free flights when you sign up to them. Normally you have to spend an X amount during a particular period which then entitles you to claim for a free return international flight. There are many other perks, like you can earn an air mile on every £1 you spend on your credit card, and if you spend a particular amount every calendar month, you could earn an additional flight ticket for your friend or a family member. I'm not an expert in this area but many people on the internet are, if you're interested in going along this route I can highly recommend the frequent flyer master program which can earn you up to 200,000 miles every year. Here's the link:

www.frequentflyermaster.com

The program allows you to try it out with a no hassle return policy and starts at $1. It's a wonderful program to try out with no strings attached to get you earning Air miles. There are Air miles just sitting there waiting to be claimed so try it out for yourself and see how far you can get.

Chapter Eighteen: Train Tricks and Rail Passes

Travelling by train can be a wonderful way to see many parts of the world, sit back and enjoy it all as it passes by your passenger seat window. It can be the slowest option but can be affordable in many cases and also an entertaining form of transportation in itself. In Europe within a matter of hours you can experience the mountains of Switzerland and then you go through a tunnel and you're experiencing the Italian vineyards up on the hills. Sceneries interchange and travel can be exciting by train.

Take the Trans-Siberian railway which travels right across Russia and even into Mongolia or China which can be a great way to break up an overland journey and grab a flight at the other end to the next destination.

For the best up-to-date resource on travelling around the world via rail, I highly recommend this website which I have used a lot over the years:

www.seat61.com

Seat61 is a hobby website set up by a passionate independently run travel enthusiast who has spent a lot of time gathering global information about taking the train around the world. The information has always been informative and correct, it's just all on there and a terrific travelling tool of a website, so do check it out. If you want to find out which seat is the best on the Eurostar or how to get to Casablanca in Morocco from Madrid in Spain this is the website for you.

Prices

Rail can be expensive in some countries and it can be cheaper to either take the bus or fly instead. Germany for example is very expensive unless you're a local and have discount passes, but still it's very expensive to use the train and so the buses can be cheaper. But for countries such as the Czech Republic it costs peanuts and is very easy to use, so see if the train is the best method for you on your adventure route. One way of making train travel affordable is by buying a rail pass for multiple days, here are a few pass examples:

Rail Passes

Rail passes can offer an affordable alternative to mass travelling options. If you plan on seeing a lot of places over a small amount of time then a rail pass can earn its weight in gold. Rail passes are discounted heavily for visitors and can allow you to explore large amounts of space in a very small time frame. Here are some examples of passes you can acquire:

Japan Rail pass

www.japantravel.co.uk/japan-rail-pass

WARNING you must purchase the pass in your home country months before you embark on your trip and you cannot purchase the pass on arrival within Japan.

Japan has one of the world's best train networks with high speed bullet trains on offer and frequent connectivity all across Japan. This makes travelling by railway a very exciting adventure with these types of trains on offer and with the frequent connectivity all across Japan. This makes travelling by railway in Japan a very exciting adventure if given the opportunity. Sadly, its very expensive but thanks to the Japan rail pass it's very possible for tourists to make rail travel affordable.

An example of how much it can cost: 2nd class, 21 days within a month, Adult: £451.00

This works out roughly to £22 a day for railway tickets. The price may look expensive on the whole, but you really can go where ever you want in Japan by rail with its well connected routes, even all the way up to the Northern Hokkaido area which would be expensive to reach without the pass. With good planning and planning the days wisely you can cover a large amount of Japan very cheaply. As an example, a one-way ticket from Tokyo to Kyoto by bullet train could cost you £100+ alone, so 4 of these trips can almost cover the cost of the pass. Just putting it into perspective.

European Rail Pass

Inter-rail pass (European residents)

www.interrail.eu

Eurail pass (Non European residents)

www.eurail.com

The most popular of all the railway passes. It's also been around the longest and used by the most. With this pass you're able to visit a total of 30 countries with the global pass. This unlocks a world of opportunities as you're free to whizz around Europe at one affordable price.

A price example: 1 month £396, Youth 2nd class. Roughly £14 a day. (Price depending on nationality)

Europe is a small continent but full of countries and railway can open possibilities up when travelling around this area. It is possible to fly but with some countries being so close to each other it would be silly sometimes when you can easily hop over a border on a train. The Interrail/Eurail pass is a very popular way to travel around Europe, and you will be arriving straight into the centre of many amazing cities. You really can do it day-in-day-out as these countries are not that far apart from each other.

Other passes to look into: Australia rail pass, Canada rail pass, Korean rail pass, South Africa rail pass, Vietnam rail pass, New Zealand rail pass.

For all the above passes they may at first look like a great deal (they most probably are!). But do look at your route and time frame first and see if the pass fits into your itinerary, because you might be able to save money by booking the tickets individually along the way when you want.

As an example for cheaper destinations such as Lithuania where train tickets might work out cheaper than the day rate of the pass (based on the all Europe destination Inter-rail pass). Might be better off using the pass for the more expensive destinations such as Germany, then purchasing the single tickets in the more affordable areas. You could also break up the pass and buy individual region specific passes which is possible such as the Eastern European Rail pass for the cheaper areas of Europe, they are better price matched.

Another point to bring up is to avoid spending a week in one city, you wont get any value out of having the pass. Every day your not travelling the pass becomes more expensive. Your better off using the pass as often as possible to use it for its full value.

This might not be the ideal way of travelling so make sure your prepared to use the pass to gain as much out of it as possible.

Chapter Nineteen: Bus About

Don't dismiss buses they can be a real money saver. In South East Asia it's very possible to travel all around by buses and can be a very affordable method of transportation. Take Malaysia for example, where the journeys can be up to 8 hours long. For around £20 you can go from Singapore right into the city centre of Kula Lumpur over night on a peaceful sleeper bed/chair which also includes a meal and movie entertainment. It can be a great alternative to flying and you can see some of the country as you pass by.

Same goes for South America where you will soon discover chicken buses are the most affordable and the easiest way to get around. Chicken buses coined there name by being the chosen transport of the local people and they tend to travel with there chickens, i.e. you might be sitting next to a cage of chickens for 10 hours, the fun of travelling hey!

In North America you will find Megabus and Greyhound are head to head on cheap prices to whisk you around to all the awesome cities to visit. In Europe check out Euro-line which has good youth prices.

Chapter Twenty: Driving Around

If you can drive, you're in for some advantages. Buying a cheap car in some countries can pay off in the long run. One great example of this is in Australia where there are a whole load of junky styled cars going up and down the Gold Coast and being sold to the next adventurer upon arrival in Sydney. Australia is massive and the roads are open and go all the way up the coast which makes it perfect for driving. Also there are a lot of places to sleep which are catered towards people who are driving, such as campsites with parking by the beach. All along the Australian coastlines there are rental BBQ's on offer and camping sites so it makes it perfect for this type of travelling. Don't forget the endless amount of beaches you can have a quick bath in as well.

Renting

Maybe you meet a group of friends at a hostel in San Diego and they are heading to Las Vegas together and they ask if you want to chip in for a rental car. Some destinations work out really well for this like in the USA where car rental is very affordable and easy to drive. San Diego to Las Vegas is a great example as they have plenty of drop off points and it will only cost you the price of one day's rental plus petrol split 5 ways. That could work out to not a lot and might even work out cheaper than the bus. So if you're travelling with friends or make new friends along the way, rentals could be a lot cheaper than the other alternatives.

Places in South East Asia rent very affordable mopeds for the day and sometimes you might be able to drive them to the next city. This can be a fun way to experience South East Asia as there is a popular moped culture. But just like the above, make sure you have all the correct papers and driving license with you before you start thinking about renting.

Its also a very good idea to inspect and take pictures of the moped before you take off. This way any fake claims that the bike wasn't damaged before you departed can easily become a thing of the past and you won't be taken for a ride yourself.

Chapter Twenty One: Accommodation

We all get tired and good rest is one of the important elements of travelling. But before you search for a hotel and get shocked by prices, please let me show you the way to hack your accommodation.

You're in luck, as there are plenty of options that work well in different locations around the world. I'll use my knowledge to better highlight all of these alternatives and to prepare you for your best option. Hotels are an option but not your only one; there are many alternatives to save yourself money. Here is the how-to travel hack with regards to accommodation:

General service hacks to save money

Wifi

Never pay for wifi. It's a pet hate of mine that hostels still charge for wifi when it really doesn't cost a lot of money to run free internet for customers. Pretty much all you're going to do is tell your friends back home about where you are and how the place is that you're staying in (giving them free advertisement!). Boycott places that don't have free wifi and they will quickly learn. A lot of places do offer free wifi and that's great! Even if it's just in the lobby, that's a progressive bonus and very awesome; good for them! But if you do get caught short, try and ask where you can get it for free. Many coffee shops or fast food restaurants offer free wifi these days and you can log on to get your fix. Avoid this expense as it can quickly add up and cost a fortune.

Breakfast

Never pick a place to stay because it has free breakfast. Breakfast from the street doesn't cost a lot and it can be rather fun to go out and have breakfast how the locals have it. Hostels/hotels that include free breakfast could be offering you anything and it might not be a great deal after all. One hotel I stayed at in Vietnam was just offering a weird soup and nothing looked very appetizing, they just put it there because it cost them nothing and they could attract breakfast hungry guests after a buffet.

A lot of hostels will translate free breakfast to mean chucking a loaf of bread and strawberry jam down every morning. Hardly what you were after right? My best advice, budget £2 a morning and go out for breakfast, get a nice coffee and cake and there you go, something different every morning.

I've had some very affordable breakfasts around the world from Kaya toast in Singapore to American pancakes and coffee in New York City, why let the hotel/hostel decide your breakfast? Buy what you want somewhere else.

Of course if it's there and it looks good, eat it. Just don't plan to hope for it that's all. Don't be put off by a hotel room for not offering breakfast, that's my point.

Chapter Twenty Two: Hostels

Hostels are perfect for solo travellers and normally come with a perfect budget price. It all comes down to the competition in the area, the size of the room on offer, and the facilities that are available. Picking a hostel can be a tough business, so I'm here to help

Not only can the price be the selling point, hostels can be very sociable as well and can attract the right type of first time travellers that you want to socialize with. This can be great for people arriving for the first time and looking for fun people to travel with to the next destination.

The most worrying thing for first time travellers can be travelling alone. But just stop for a moment and think. So many backpackers are in many major cities right now, talking over a beer in one of the many thousands of hostels. Now with that in mind travelling to your next destination tomorrow isn't too much of a shock as there are already travellers at the hostel you are heading to who are waiting to meet you over a beer in the evening.

The coolest thing about this hostel culture is you meet people who are either going where you're next going, or have already just been there. So hostels are great for planning trips in, and the staff there are used to the endless amount of questions that people have as they have heard them again and again. These people tend to know the perfect answer; in fact they are pro at it and are happy to help.

Hostels can be very social places and can help you ease into travel.

Here is some advice on how to book a hostel.

First step get a 'Hostelling International' membership card. They are very affordable, last a long time and can get you discounts during your stay and unlock a network of hostels all around the world in some unique locations. Hostelling International is a charity which has been helping travellers out for many years. They actually have very helpful staff and information on their website. You don't have to always stay with them but their hostels always meet a standard that they have to live up to, so when booking a hostel at Hostel International you can always be reassured of the level of service that they will provide all around the world.

www.hihostels.com

Two great hostel booking websites:

www.hostelworld.com

www.hostelbookers.com

With these two hostel bookers along with HI you're pretty much covered for every hostel in the world.

Hostelworld and Hostelbookers are equally as good and are set up differently so it all comes down to your own personal choice and what you prefer to use.

Hostelbookers is free, while Hostelworld requires a small yearly fee (however it's rather easy to find a free 6 month trail on Google). I prefer the design and layout and ease of use from Hostelworld but this is my personal opinion and you should have a look at both and play around to see what you think of both sites.

But I must warn you that just because it's a hostel, it doesn't mean it's cheap. Sometimes hotels can be more affordable depending on where you are and what time of year it is. Always shop around and compare the alternatives, especially when you're looking for a place to stay for more than one person.

How to pick the perfect hostel

This also relates to how to pick any accommodation with a review option on offer. I'm just going to use Hostels as an example. Points to look out for:

Price

The reason why you have chosen to stay at a hostel over a hotel is the price. Maybe you will consider the social aspects, but mostly you're looking at the price. Some hostels are now rather expensive, but don't let this put you off as you can still find a bargain. How many beds in your room will determine the price point of the hostel. I have stayed in a room with 48 beds in it before and it felt like I was on an army base but it was very affordable. Some people can manage a 10 bed dorm room, whilst others can't. You need to work out what's best for your comfort level. If you're like me and you don't care, then the more people there are, the cheaper it is; awesome. Many will be able to manage a 6 to 8 person dorm. This will of course affect the cost, but one hostel with 6 bed dorms might charge the same as the hostel over the road which is offering a 10 dorm so do shop around.

Location

It might look great in the photos but if it's an hour walk from the centre, it might not be the location for you. Some cities are massive, so location might not be an issue. Take Sydney for example; there are loads of different areas where hostels are located. Kings Cross is a popular backpacker area in Sydney, as that is where the night life is, but there is also the Sydney central station which is another hostel area and is completely on the other side of town. Bondi beach again is a boat ride away and has a few hostels as well. You want to work out what you're doing and then find the best location to suit your needs. It's normal for hostels to be located all over the place, so ask people on the road where they stayed and jot them down for when you're in that town in the future. That way you're then prepared to look up places to stay when you get there.

Social life

You can normally get a picture of what the vibe will be like by looking at the photos and the reviews. Some hostels are designed for parties, whilst others are designed for quiet sleeping. Judge the hostel yourself and decide if you want to party or if you want to sleep, as you can have two different experiences. What's really annoying is reading on the site that pub crawls will take place and then seeing people complaining on there that it was noisy. You're smart and can put the two together. Don't knock a hostel if they want to party and they make a noise, some backpackers are only after this. Of course this goes for party animals as well, don't go for a sleepy backpacker if you want to rave to the early hours of the morning. People have to grab flights in the morning respect backpacker's choices.

Reputation

I stayed at one backpacker that was famous for guests flashing their asses every night at the cars passing by. I did not know this till I read the reviews online on the booking website after I stayed there. Make sure that you read up on places as some hostels have a reputation for crime, theft or drugs and you don't want to wander into a situation like that. Read reviews and draw a picture of the place you're staying. Not all Hostels are bad, but sadly there are a few that shouldn't be in operation, so be careful.

Facilities

You're going to be paying extra for facilities so make sure you're going to be using them. I stayed at a hostel once because it had very good free airport shuttle busses on offer. It was Dubai, and I was using it as a stopover, so the shuttle bus was perfect and just what I needed to have a good sleep. It saved me sleeping on the airport floor. If you need something, choose the hostel for that purpose and not for its other facilities. Hostels will charge extra for the Playstation room and the swimming pool as the other hostels don't have them and they can charge extra for it. However, this is funny because sometimes it seems that a karaoke salesman goes around all the hostels selling the machines telling them the other hostels have them so you should get one too. Luckily, this is the case and a lot of facilities are standard in hostels (free wifi!) but if you're not going to use the swimming pool don't pay extra for it, go to a cheaper hostel.

Reviews

Reviews are very helpful to get an overview from a staying guest rather than the biography that the hotel itself has written about it. This is because customer generated feedback is more helpful in creating an image of what you really want to find out rather than what is expected. You can learn quickly what kind of a place it is from past guests reviews as they will tell you how it really is and this will help you with your booking.

Don't be fooled by reviews, just because a hostel has 100% doesn't make it better than the hostel with 71% you need to take many things into consideration. How many reviews does it have, where are the review makers from and how many of the reviews are saying the same thing. 20 positive reviews at

71% is better than 2 at 100%, as it's more broad with its feedback.

Nationality of the reviewer helps as we all demand different things and are used to different levels of comfort. One person's paradise is another's disaster, so bare this in mind when searching. Normally reviews from first time travellers are a lot different as well as they are not used to shared showers or large hostel rooms yet and you can normally pick out the seasoned travellers from the newbies who will give you a better picture.

You can also use other review websites to do some further background checking rather than relying on the booking website alone. One resource I use is www.Tripadvisor.com. It's good to check for reviews here as people are more likely to leave them compared to on the actual hostel website or the booking website.

But do be warned as people are more than likely to leave a negative review than a positive review so positive reviews should be seen as higher than negative reviews or no reviews at all. This is just the way it is, it takes a lot to make someone leave a review but it's very easy for an unhappy customer to spill everything out negatively. So do bear this in mind and really appreciate positive reviews.

Sometimes hostels have negative reviews from when they first opened or during a particular management spell so it's best to separate current reviews from recent guests from reviews made a couple of years ago.

Also, don't give a place a hard time if they have negative reviews about bed bugs. You normally find that it was a large influx of negatives that happened a while ago and they have dealt with the issue since then. All hostels have had bedbugs, they happen, but they get dealt with quickly once discovered. Unless the comments are from recent times, then I wouldn't worry about them too much, they have probably all been eliminated.

When you stay at a place be sure to leave a review when you leave to help out the next guest as it is really helpful to your fellow travellers and it doesn't take too much of your time.

Chapter Twenty Three: Hotels

Sometimes hotels can be the easiest and cheapest options. Don't presume hostels are always the answer because it's simply not the case. It really varies city to city. One great example is Las Vegas. Hotels in Las Vegas rarely sell all of their hotel rooms. In fact, this normally only happens a few times a year, which is mostly when the big annual Expo's are in town and apart from these events a lot of the hotel rooms stay empty. If you pick a not so busy time and pay well in advance you can stay in some of the nicest hotels along the strip for a fraction of the buy-on-the-day price. And as for the low market hotels along the strip, you can apply the same process but at a rock bottom price. Not only this, but if you ask nicely for an upgrade it might just happen. Las Vegas is hotel city and the staff are allowed to upgrade guests for many reasons, so all you have to do is ask nicely and see what happens.

This doesn't work in all cities, but it's just an example of how it can work out and how it's best to shop around for alternatives. There are only a few hostels in Las Vegas and I stayed in the Stratosphere once for a cheaper price than what the hostel was asking, so there you have it!

But if you're travelling with an extra friend or as a couple, you most likely want to look into budget hotels anyway as private rooms in hostels can be very expensive and are often not up to the standard of hotel rooms. They get you in because you think it's cheap, but actually a hotel might have worked out better.

The biggest mistake is to think of the big chains when looking at hotels. There are plenty of wonderful budget hotels that attract the family market as well as the growing holiday-makers market in areas around Europe and Asia.

One example of this is www.TuneHotel.com Run and owned by the large South East Asian budget airline

AirAsia, Tune hotel operate very close to where they fly, making it easy for you to book flights and hotels with them. Just like the airline they are very affordable but designed for those on a budget. You have to pay for many of the extra aspects in the hotel (e.g. towel/TV/hair-drier), but the double bed and hot shower are included for a low price and I have stayed with them in Malaysia for as low as £4 a night.

Just like the above, there are many examples of this kind of low budget hotel around the world and sometimes they work out cheaper than a hostel, so it's best to shop around and see what you can find.

Chapter Twenty Four: Alternative Sleeps

Pod hotels

If you travel around Japan you can try out something quite unique to this part of the world; a capsule/pod hotel. Pod hotels were designed mostly for Japanese businessmen who missed the last train home and need a cheap place to stay for the night. However, they have grown very popular among backpackers looking for an affordable sleep. Designed to house a lot of people in a very small amount of space, pod hotels can be a very enjoyable experience for travellers to try out as they are so unique.

If you would like to look at an example of a perfect one that I stayed at for a very affordable price in the centre of Kyoto, here is the '9 hour' hotel: www.9hours.jp.

Normally, you will be supplied with disposable soap and toothpaste along with a pair of slippers. Some pods even supply bed PJ's as well as the bedding (because it's normally people who miss the train that use them they don't have anything for the night's sleep) but it is also a Japanese custom to supply such things in hotels.

Also bathing is commonly in a large hot tub area (onsen) and you bathe together with other guests. Because of this, quite often these capsule hotels are split in half for males and females.

Pod hotels can be an affordable way to travel around Japan and work really well with the Japanese rail pass which is explained in the train section of this book. They are both weird and unique and should be tried if given the opportunity when in Japan.

I have also seen them in Amsterdam (www.Yotel.com) as well as London so they are catching on in the Western world as well.

Sleep at the airport

www.Sleepinginairports.net

Let's face it; a lot of the cheaper flights will be very early in the morning at around 6am. This makes it ridiculous to book a hotel for a night as you have to wake up extremely early anyway and then make it from the hotel to the airport. It's just not worth booking a hotel at all. Use the sleepinginairports.net website to check if you can sleep overnight in the terminal. Most airports are 24 hour operations and never close. I have contributed to the website a lot over the years and find the information offered to be a great resource.

The best trick is to arrive at midnight (normally when the last flights take off). Lock your bags up in the lockers, or check them in early if possible and then find somewhere to rest your head for the next 4 hours. When it's time for your flight you can sleep on the flight, simple.

Warning! Some airports close at night or kick out sleepers, so best to check the website to see if this is the case. Some airports are extremely friendly though, like in Milan, I pitched my tent there and was not disturbed for 6 hours, perfect! I also found a free coffee machine and WIFI, all thanks to the website.

Sleep on the way

Have you ever thought about sleeping whilst you travel? Some distances can be rather long and with night journeys and sleeper options why not cut the cost of accommodation into your travels. A lot of routes offer this service for example if you're travelling from London to Scotland (which is a good 8 hour journey) you can take the www.Megabus.com service which offers a sleeper bed, and I've even seen the fare for as low as £1! Also, if you have a rail pass such as the Inter Rail pass, some of the sleeper routes just require a reservation and won't cost you anything extra. I've travelled from the North of Japan (Sapporo) down to Tokyo whilst I slept, which was wonderful waking up and having breakfast in a capital city without any time lost at all.

Sleeping on the bus/train/boat and travelling overnight can save you both time and money. It's extremely smart so consider this as an option.

Camping

Now this option is based on two points:

1) You will have to lug your own tent and extra equipment around

2) It's weather permitting.

However, it can be a very rewarding way to sleep whilst on your travels. In the summer it can be a great way of getting around Europe, to make the most out of the sun and lovely green fields, and can be an alternative to staying in expensive hotels.

Did you know that all of Finland/Norway/Sweden have a law stating that you can pitch and sleep where ever you want as long as you clean up after yourself in public places? Even a lot of private landowners in these areas don't mind you camping as long as you have a polite word with them first and don't hang around for too long.

It was one of the most magical highlights when travelling around this area, just pitching your tent up by a fjord on a hill and cooking dinner then getting some sleep under the midsummer sky. I pitched my tent all over the Nordic area and found it most fun. The whole time no one bothered me or told me to move, maybe a few dogs running up to my tent to say hello, but no-one had anything against what I was doing and it was fantastic.

Yes you have to bring and lug around a tent as well as cooking equipment but in areas such as the Nordics were it can cost £100 a night in a hotel and with no hostels in sight, this can be a wonderful option.

Also, for camping in places such as the UK or America you might not even have to lug around a tent as some campsites rent out tents for a small fee, this can be great for locations such as London where it's expensive to stay but have plenty of campsites on the outskirts that rent out low rate tents for a few nights, and can be a bit of an adventure as well.

Cabins in the woods

A lot of hiking spots or cities with campsites also have cheap cabins that you can rent, these are normally reached by walking or by bus. Normally they work on a 'first come first trust' system where you leave what you want to pay in a jar before you clean up and leave. This can be very fun in many places such as Iceland where it's very popular to do this method. I've seen them located in Australia and Canada as well and so these can be a fun alternative for a place to stay as they are normally rather cheap.

Chapter Twenty Five: House Share

Renting

When stuck looking for a cheap hotel/hostel in Melbourne I become a little stuck. I have always wanted to hang around Melbourne as it's such a fun city and I wanted to experience it long term. For the price of a 3 night hotel stay I managed to rent a place for a whole month. How? Well in cities where it's popular to study many students will go home for a holiday period such as Easter break and many people list their rooms for short term renting. Not only this, but some Flat rental companies are happy to rent out for a month or three if demand is running a little low. This also works out well for hotel apartments and normally many hotels/hostels will have a month rate as well as a daily rate so you can look around and see what's available there.

You can ask around friends if they know anyone who is going home for the holidays or have a spare room in their student house, you could even email student rental agencies and see if they have anything during the holidays. Many students are asked to clear their rooms during busy holiday periods so they can offer student halls for travellers looking for an affordable place to stay.

Staying put in a city for a month or longer really changes the way you experience that city and some places are better explored long term. It's also very nice to hang your boots for a while sometimes and catch up on your to-do lists or just to allow yourself to kick back and not have to move in the next week.

I found when living in a city for longer than a month you start to become a local and you experience the city in a completely different way. This can be exciting in its self and can be a fun adventure on your trip.

Not only this but you could pick yourself up an affordable bargain if you get the right price as rent is a lot cheaper than hotel rooms over a period of time.

Places to look for renting:

www.Airbnb.com

www.craigslist.com

www.Couchsurfing.org > city sub groups.

Home stay

www.trustedhousesitters.com

Looking for a free place to stay in return for a little work? Many people that go on holiday for one or two weeks have a pet that they need someone to look after and to keep an eye on their house whilst their gone. This can be a great way to bag free accommodation for a long period of time almost anywhere in the world. All you have to do is some light housework, keep an eye on the property while the owners are away and feed/walk the pet. It's very simple to do with great returns on accommodation savings. Sometimes the properties don't even have any pets at all and the owner just wants someone to secure the property and keep an eye on it whilst they are away which can be an option if you have an allergy to pets.

Flat Share

A new way is emerging with regards to holiday accommodation. People are starting to open up their homes to travellers for a price. Locals are turning themselves into hotel receptionists by offering their own home as a hotel. In many cases this has helped locals who have apartments in popular cities that are just sitting there and doing nothing by allowing them to make a steady flow of cash for themselves. However, other locals who are still living in their house are offering a spare room for visitors to rent at a small price. This is great in areas where rent is high and hotel prices are as well, such as Hong Kong or New York City. Locals can then offer what they can to help travellers out and help themselves in return with the profit they make. I think it's a great idea and you get to experience what a local home is like as well as saving much needed travel money.

Websites to check out:

www.AirBnb.com

www.homeaway.com

Chapter Twenty Six: Home Hospitality

Remember that one guy you worked with from Brazil? Still have his contact details? Can you cast your mind back to that Singaporean you met at the football game who said he would love to show you around his city if you were ever to visit? Use what you have.

The world is a very small place and the connections that we make last a lifetime. If you're lucky enough to have met someone from another country and you remember them well, there is a big chance that they will remember you too, be cheeky and ask if they want to meet up as there is a big chance that they will want to. You will never know if you never ask, the worst they can say is 'no. sorry I'm busy', so what do you have to lose?

When you live a normal 9-5 work week, having someone visit from overseas can make you look at things differently and you become a tourist in your own city. That's why it's a fun idea to see if your international friends are open to meeting up, and if you're lucky, maybe they'll have a free place for you to stay as well. This is a great opportunity to see how different cultures live and to experience a different way of life.

So keep hold of those international contacts, you never know when you might be visiting them.

If you're a part of a worldwide club or organization see if there are any members who live overseas and see if they would like to meet up. It's very common that people who have shared interests get along well, so that's why clubs and associations are great for this as you have something in common.

For example, I'm a scout and have met up with many international scouts on my travels as we share the same interests and it's great to catch up and share scouting experience with each other even though we do scouting in different countries.

Couchsurfing

Couchsurfing is much more than a method used for free accommodation, it's much more than that; it's a community.

I have been using Couchsurfing ever since I started travelling and I will remember my first couch experience for a very long time as well as all the other endless amounts of amazing couches, people and experiences I have encountered whilst using the project.

www.Couchsurfing.org puts travellers and people who live in the local communities together. It allows you to network and share your culture by offering whatever you have to share with people.

For a large majority that like to use the project, they will offer their couch for the night, maybe even a spare room if they have it or a blow up mattress or some floor space. Some prefer to just meet up for a coffee and a conversation or maybe even half a day of sightseeing around their city or maybe even a meal. Lots of endless possibilities and every Couchsurfing experience will be a different one.

For me travelling is about the people you meet and Couchsurfing offers that gateway directly into a local person's life. You can see how someone lives their life differently, culturally and socially, and you learn way faster about the local culture than you would reading a book, or exploring the city.

The rare chance to step into a locals shoes and see the place your visiting through their unique eyes. You could visit the same city and have a totally different experience whilst using Couchsurfing. I think its bloody brilliant!

Rules to help you have a better Couchsurfing experience

First time Couchsurfing can be tricky and confusing, as you have to learn a lot very fast. Once you get into the swing of things you unlock many great future Couchsurfing experiences for the future to come. Here are some tips on how to make your experience incredible.

Fill out your profile

Very important. When Couchsurfers gather requests they want to get to know what you're about as a person. Hosts don't just host everyone because they are friendly they generally want to meet people they can connect with to make the experience enjoyable on both ends. Filling out your profile will attract people who share the same interests as you. This might even be the languages you speak or the places you have travelled to.

Upload pictures

Upload a bunch of recent pictures of yourself doing things you love and visiting the places you said you have been to. People want to see what you look like and if they can match your pictures up with what you're saying then trust comes into the picture and helps hosts to feel good about putting you up. They can also inspire talking points for your future meeting. Couchsurfers love to talk, so photos help break the ice when it comes to bringing up topics to talk about.

Be alert

Don't just send requests out to everyone, read their profiles as well and check them out. It's just as important that you understand the person you're messaging as much as it is for them to find out stuff about you. Avoid hosts that don't have photos or much information on their profiles and check if they have had past guest and referrals to backup that they are good people. Just because they are offering a couch doesn't mean that they have good intentions. A large majority of Couchsurfers are good people, but it doesn't automatically mean everyone is. Read up on the people you request and make sure you're comfortable and satisfied that you like them well enough to message them.

Send personal messages

Don't send copy and paste messages to hosts as they will just ignore you, make it personal. Write about what you read in their profile and what they have in common with you that you like and let them know that you have read their profile. It shows that you have taken the time to do it and will make it a fun Couchsurfing experience for the both of you.

Arrive prepared

Demanding everything on arrival is horrible, bring along your own bedding and towel and mention this in the email, hosts will be grateful that they don't have to worry about you and you can look after yourself. Helping out the host in this way makes it easier for them to agree with your hosting request as they don't have to worry about a lot of things if they don't have them. But a lot of the time they will be happy to share towels and sheets if they have them, just don't expect them as it comes across as rude.

Don't be seen, be heard.

You will most likely be sleeping in the host's social area on the couch, which means that they can't use that room if you're using it. Be mindful of this and respect the host's space. Every morning wake up when the host wakes up and fold your sheets and put them away neatly so it's out of the way and the room is usable. Don't dominate all their space and make them feel unwelcome in their own home. It's not your home so respect this and make it clear that you don't want to take over their house, they will get along with you so much better if you do. This is the same for your bag, so make sure you pack everything up again after use and don't leave everything all over the floor.

Smelly backpacker's syndrome

If you smell and you know it, ask your host nicely when you arrive if you can freshen up and apologise whilst saying you've been on the road. This is very polite as it shows you want to be nice and presentable around the host and your host's friends. If you smell and don't say anything it can be uncomfortable for the person hosting you. If you highlight it they will completely understand as it's what happens when you travel and respect you for wanting to deal with it. Many hosts will also offer the use of laundry if you want to clean clothes but don't expect it. Wanting to be clean in their house is very polite and they are normally very happy to offer the use of a shower.

Never expect anything

Be grateful for whatever your host can offer. If it is just a space on the floor then so be it, be prepared for it and don't complain. They are not a hotel and are going out of their way to help you out. If they do have a spare bed, great! And be grateful to them for doing that for you as well, they don't have to put that on for you.

Arrange a meeting?

If you arrange to meet up make sure you are not only on time but early, leaving a Couchsurfer waiting for you is incredibly rude. Also make sure you leave enough information and have an easy to reach phone number available to make contacting each other easy.

Come prepared

The worst thing you can do is arrive at a host's place and have nothing to do. It comes across as if you're just staying with them for no reason. We all have ideas of what we want to do in the places we visit, so make sure you have a few suggestions up your sleeve. The best thing you can say is 'I was hoping for some unique things to do that only locals know about', along with your few suggestions this will help make it easier for your host to come up with some fun things to do and help you to get along.

Be able to be independent

Some people can only offer a couch overnight and will have work during the day. Always suggest that you're happy to be alone and to do your own thing. Make sure that you're up and out of the house with them so they are not late for work as that would be horrible. Also use the toilet room quickly so you're not holding them up when they are preparing for work, this helps to make them feel happy they are hosting you and not stressing them out by making them late for work. If they do work, meeting up for a meal or drink when they finish can give your host something exciting to look forward to during the day, so do suggest this.

Food and drink

Never under any situation expect that you will get food. Always pay your way for everything and if anything is offered be very grateful for the host for doing such a thing. If you go to buy food, offer to help pay for items or go Dutch with the shopping bill. It's just as polite as they shouldn't be paying for you as they are doing a lot as it is. But if they say 'please, no it's not a problem I'm happy to pay', don't keep pushing them to pay, just be thankful for the food they are providing and preparing for you. You can always offer to cook the next day which is a nice gesture.

When out drinking I always offer to buy my host a drink and the same goes for museum fees or bus tickets. They are taking you out and being a guide, so the least you can do is offer to pay for their things, especially the tourist attractions. Again, if they want to pay for themselves, don't force it, just offer the polite gesture in the first place. You don't want to offend people because they might get the impression that you think they can't afford to pay for themselves, which can be offensive in some cultures, but offering first time won't offend anyone.

Give them something at the end

It's always polite to say thank you to your host when you leave. They have just let you stay at their place for free and I'm sure you have both had a memorable experience. You don't have to shell out on a bottle of wine every time you Couchsurf (of course you're very welcome to if it's in your nature to do so and you're happy to do it, it's a lovely gesture). But even a box of chocolates, a nice thoughtful letter, or maybe even an offer to cook one night as a thank you gift. Be creative and give something back, it will make them remember you and they will feel grateful inside for you doing such an awesome thing.

Always offer to host back

Couchsurfing is not a one-way project, you should give back too. Hosting can be a wonderful thing to do after travelling around the world and you miss meeting new people and learning about new cultures, so why not do it in your own place and host travellers that come to you? Also, always offer your hosts to come and visit and stay in your city if they ever pass by, it's the least you can do for their travels and will make them host more people in the future.

Always leave reviews

It's a very polite thing to do and spend as much time as you can to write a nice long message as it helps future Couchsurfers when finding a host and makes the host feel good for hosting you in the first place.

Starting out

When you first start Couchsurfing you're going to find it hard to find your first couch so do make sure you write a nice message to the host and fill out your profile with lots of updated pictures. I'm sure someone will host you if they find you interesting and have the time. Stick at it, as it's tricky to find your first host but once you have a good 10 reviews from successful surfing experiences it will open the door to many more opportunities in the future.

Chapter Twenty Seven: Food for Thought

On my travels I have eaten in some amazing places and tried some incredible foods. The wonderful thing about travel is how food can be so different everywhere you go. I have also eaten with locals at hawker markets, eaten street food and tried some crazy dishes such as crocodile testicles. The funny thing is after eating at all these locations (even in India!) there was only one place that I have felt ill from eating. That happened to be close to home at a popular fast food restaurant which happened to be located in Swansea, Wales. It was a bit of a shock but it just goes to show you that even when eating down the road at home you are at risk so it doesn't matter about all these new dishes you want to try, just enjoy the experience.

Here are some tips to help you be frugal when it comes to buying food on the road:

Set meals

Set meals are also offered at a lot of places such as 3 course meals for $9.99, eat all you like buffets or Beer and Burger combo deal at the pub, look out for offers and see what you can find, anything you can save is an added bonus. Many places will offer cut prices during quiet times in order to gain customers. In Hong Kong a trend that is growing is affordable brunch menus, a mixture of lunch and breakfast for those looking for a sleep-in and cheap eats.

Coupons

Many restaurants offer discount coupons and they can easily be located online within such websites such as: www.vouchercloud.com. I always have a quick Google to see what I can find and normally you gather 20% off your total bill which is an added bonus. Also, growing in popularity is Foursquare, a check-in application that can offer discounts for customers who have used the application at the said location. They are marked with a special discount logo which is easy to spot once you have checked-in on the application.

Happy hours

Happy hours can also be found at many hostels and backpacker bars which are looking to pull you in with cheap beer and chicken wings. Well why not make the most of what is on offer. Some hostels will even give you free drinks upon check-in just to make you check out the bar area, use what you get.

Avoid tourist hotspots

Do you know that restaurants in Venice charge you based on the location in which you are sitting and the view you are experiencing and not the food? Exactly. Head out of town a little and find somewhere a little quieter. If you fancy the view it's free to sit on a bench with a packed lunch, no one will move you.

If it's busy it's normally a good sign

With so many places offering food on your travel it can be very confusing to find the perfect place. My rule of thumb is if it has a massive line then it's worth the time. If it's empty during a busy time there is a reason for this so avoid empty places and head to where the locals are buzzing around. In Japan this really helped as 10 places in one area would be selling the same thing but some places would fill up whilst some remained empty. Joining the busy places never disappointed me once and I always had top notch meals. So there you go, it does work.

End of the day

In the UK this works a treat and I've found it to be handy in many other locations. Visit cafes and supermarkets close to closing time and fresh food is normally marked up at a discount before it's sent to the bin. You might be able to find some healthy eats for a rock bottom price.

Try street food

Don't immediately cross out street food, it can be both enjoyable and affordable at the same time. It's also a great place to mingle and meet the locals as this is often the hang out spot of choice for many. Real traditional local food can be found here and you won't find it better anywhere else at the price it's on offer for.

Avoid Meat and dairy in high risk locations

Before travelling to India I was told by many people to be careful not to catch any food illnesses. One rule I learned quickly was to eat like the locals and go vegetarian. Vegetarian food in India was some of the best food I've ever tasted and was extremely affordable as well. Meat is high risk and if not cooked properly could cause you a lot of problems. Avoiding it can really help you from not getting ill. But with vegetarian food being so tasty it really won't be a problem to leave out meat for a few weeks. Dairy is also high risk and should be avoided in India, stick to evaporated milk for tea, which is always used by locals.

Use your water bottle!

You packed it, so use it. Avoid expensive soda and stick to the good stuff that comes out of the tap for free, you'll be saving yourself a fortune!

Use the hostel kitchen

If your hostel has a kitchen then use it, pick up some ingredients from the supermarket and cook yourself up a meal, if you see anyone hanging around the hostel looking hungry ask if they want to join in the fun and cut the cost between each other. I find shopping in local supermarkets to be rather enjoyable as it's a lot different to back home. You can also try and cook up a local meal as all the ingredients will be easy to find, you can ask the hostel receptionist what they recommend you to cook and ask if they wouldn't mind printing off a recipe. This can be a very fun way to cook a meal.

Preparing your lunch for the day at a hostel can really save you a lot of money compared to eating out. You'll be heading to some fun locations so they would make perfect picnic stop offs. Food is food and eating out can cost you a lot so plan this for special occasions and make it an experience when it does.

Ask a local

You're going to be faced with many great restaurant locations to eat out at on your travels. To find the best I've found it's always successful to ask a local, they will always have an opinion of a place or area to check out and this can be a great way to find a hidden gem. The popular tourist spot might not be the best place. Locals will tend to head to a different area where it can be affordable, this is how hot spots are born, which you might not have found otherwise. For example, my cousin who lives in Canada always suggests great chicken wing places to eat. In fact we always look forward to meeting up just so we can hang out and eat wings, this is Canada, the home of chicken wings. The locals will be sure to point out a hand full of top suggestions, as well as critically assess different places and varieties of orders, after all its where they live, they have had plenty of time to do this, you on the other hand have just arrived. If you want the best of the best; ask a local.

Chapter Twenty Eight: Visa Information

As a British citizen you can visit a lot of places without needing to get a visa in advance or without needing one at all. I hate visas as I feel they limit tourism and can put people off locations, not help support it. But don't let Visa's put you off travelling, if you get a lot of them, they can eat into your budget. This section is about general travel visas for visitors, go to the 'A World of Work and Study' section to find out about working visa opportunities.

As the visa requirements change a lot, please consult with the embassy in which country you are visiting for the most up-to-date prices and requirements.

I like to use a great Wikipedia page which gets updated regularly and lays out the requirements very well:

www.wikipedia.org/wiki/Visa_requirements_for_British_nationals

Also check out this site which is a little easier to understand with an interactive map and nationality selection:

www.visamapper.com

A great website for British travellers to find out about travel alerts and general information about travel can be found at the government run website:

www.gov.uk/knowbeforeyougo

Visa costs can be expensive so its important to keep these costs into account for your total trip budget as some of them can become a shock if not prepared. Generally one entry visas will cost you between £15-25. But some can cost upwards of £40 and need to be purchased in advance so use the above website maps to work this out (I would write them up but they change so frequently that the websites would be more up-to-date).

Chapter Twenty Nine: Travel Insurance

How to pick the most affordable travel insurance policy

Without travel insurance I would have had nothing, I would have just been stuck and had to bail myself out, in such situations that's the last thing you want to do. Lucky for me, I had travel insurance.

My travel insurance company of choice: World Nomads

www.worldnomads.com

But do check if you can get it for free first. Phone up your bank and see if they offer travel Insurance along with their bank accounts. I discovered that if you bank with HSBC, you can Upgrade to a student account (gap year also qualifies) which includes free travel insurance, bonus!

Travelling without travel insurance is like having sex without using a condom. It's just pure stupid. Just get it and never think about it until you have to use it.

You might see it as an annoying expense that you have to fork out for, but with multi backpacker trip policies at low prices it's silly not to.

Pick the insurance relevant to where you are travelling. If you're going to be based in Australia for one year the policy might be cheaper if it's Australia/New Zealand cover only. Also make sure that if you're not travelling to the USA to say you're not because USA travel insurance is more expensive and you can cut your final price if you're not going to travel there.

The most important part of the travel insurance, without it you have a very pointless policy. How to make sure it's a good policy? Read the small print on what it covers you for.

Make sure the cover is into the millions so you're completely covered if something bad happens. It may sound silly now but it has been known to go into this figure, make sure you're covered for this excessive amount and hope you never need that much.

One example of a past case that went into the millions:

Guy breaks his leg in a USA national park close to the Rockies. Emergency mountain rescue gets to the scene and calls out a helicopter which then drops off the patient to an ambulance which then drives to the private hospital and orders an X-Ray, then doctors are needed to look at the X-Ray. Next, he's into surgery with all the doctors doing the operations along with one week of the patient needing the hospital bed and food with many more X-rays. This is an example of a million plus claim. If you didn't have the insurance you would have to take it out from a bank and pay it back at high interest. When you have an emergency like that the doctors will not think twice about how much it will cost you they will just do it at your expense. Get travel insurance and make sure it has a good health policy. You will most probably never use it, but if you have to, you'll be very thankful you have it.

Other areas you should look into covering

Death and funeral fees, this means that if you die when travelling, your family won't have to worry about paying for an expensive flight to get your body home. It will be covered and they will have nothing to worry about. It's up to you if you want this but I get it as it makes me sleep a little easier at night knowing my family don't have to worry about a thing if that was to happen.

Excess waver

Normally the cheaper the cover the higher the waver cost is. This means for in case you have a medical emergency you may have to pay the first £200 and the rest is covered. For a £20,000 operation paying only £200 of that bill does seem like a much better deal. The higher the waver the cheaper the insurance so you have to work out yourself how much your prepared to pay up front in such situations.

Covering valuables

Once you have health covered you have the main bases of the much needed travel insurance. When it comes to expensive items however, do read the cover as it might be £1,000 for electronics as a whole and will cover in multiples of £100 per item. That means if your laptop gets stolen you will get £100 back, not the £700 it cost, so make sure this part is clear and you know exactly what you will be getting covered.

Personally I never cover electronics. I did on my first trip, but after that I realized that if my phone or laptop got stolen I would be prepared to buy a new one myself. Now I put the cost of what the policy amount would be each year into my banks saving account. Now if I did ever have these items stolen, I can cover myself (after many years of saving). If I still have my Electronics after all my travels then I have a lovely pot of beer money waiting for me at the end.

Passport and visa?

Should you cover your passport on your insurance? The cost of getting a new one will be under £100, so is it worth paying extra to cover this fee? It's up to you; I personally would just buy a new one if that was to happen.

Chapter Thirty: Health

Travel Jabs - You're going to need them so get them done; travel smart.

Before you go, please consult with your doctor and tell them where you are going to be travelling to. They can then make sure you have the correct travel jabs for that area and will check to see if you need malaria tablets or not. Doctors regularly get all the up-to-date information on what you need for which destinations. I am not a trained professional in this area so I can only tell you to seek expert advice on what you will need.

Before you leave on your trip, make sure you have a copy of all the travel jabs you have had, before you depart for your trip. Normally, your doctor will give you a special 'jab passport'. Make sure you scan it and keep a copy online loaded onto your email account, or Dropbox/Evernote, or whatever you use.

This is important as some destinations require that you provide proof that you have had the jab upon arrival. Why is this important to have the documents that you have had the jabs? Because if you can't prove it, they give it to you there and then at the border and the needles might not be safe so make sure you're prepared at the borders.

Also, it's wise to carry a compact first aid kit with you on your travels with clean needles and other medical equipment. Maybe the destination you're going to won't have clean facilities, so at least you can offer your own. They might not be able to supply these types of medical needs for their own people let alone yourself. Having your own kit might help in getting you treated if you were to have an accident.

Of course this is location specific, so make sure you consult a doctor over this method and see if this is one of the steps you might need to take. For more information about travel health and jabs, head to this helpful website from the NHS:

www.nhs.uk/conditions/Travel-immunisation

Chapter Thirty One: A world of Work & Study

Living, studying or working for a long period of time in a location can be a completely different experience compared to visiting for a few days.

This section is mostly aimed towards British passport holders, but generally can relate to other nationalities as well so don't automatically skip this section.

This section is all about stepping out of that comfort zone and giving you endless amounts of choices that almost anyone can do all around the world.

WWOOF (Woofing) - World Wide Opportunities to Organic farming

www.wwoof.org.uk

I have a funny story. When I was driving around the Rockies in Canada, my friend and I got a little lost one time until we noticed a few people on top of a roof. We pulled over and asked directions to a lodge and they were very helpful and we managed to find our way. When I asked the 6 people on top of the roof what they were doing they all replied in a German accent, "Roofing!" I was very confused at that point why 6 German people were needed in the middle of nowhere to do some roofing. I was puzzled because the roof was very small and there was so many of them, surely it was a mistake. It wasn't until a few months later I met some more Germans doing "WWOOFING" in Australia and after a few laughs over a beer I figured out that they were helping out an organic farm and not in an organisation for Germans who are good at mending roofs!

We all learn a lot from travelling and WWOOF is something you can pick up quickly as an option for getting some work whilst abroad. It's a network of easy work offered by organic farms, a lot of help is needed globally from low cost labour and backpackers are able to pick up anything from strawberry picking in the fields, to feeding animals, to general maintenance. It's not amazing pay, and in some cases you might only get food and a roof over your head for your troubles, but it's easy work and readily available. You will quickly find that a lot of other backpackers will also be working on the organic farms so it's very possible to meet and make new friends in these environments. Normally, due to farmers markets and trade associations, farms are very well linked and if you do a good job farmers are likely to pass on a recommendation to the next farm. You can unlock a lot of opportunities if go down this route, and you'll be helping out farmers who are in need of extra workers.

Great thing about WWOOF; as well is it being a global organisation that works all around the world, you never know where it might take you. In a lot of cases you might not need a working visa (depending on the work and location. Best to check into the situation before you start). In Australia by doing some farming on your working visa it's possible to get a 6 month extension for doing rural work. So if your job ends and you want to extend your time in Australia this is one option you can take.

Australia, New Zealand working visa

Australia: www.immi.gov.au/visitors/working-holiday

New Zealand: www.immigration.govt.nz/migrant/stream/work/worktemporarily

Being British you're very lucky, as long as you are under the age of 35 you can apply for a one year working visa in either Australia or New Zealand. Yep, that's correct you can do a total of 2 years (even more with a rural work extension) working in these awesome countries and all you have to do is apply.

Applying can be very easy, you can do it online and receive a response in a matter of days if you have been accepted or not. The success rate is very high but not guaranteed. It's easy because it's mostly a simple back ground check and once you're cleared you can start working in Australia & New Zealand.

Both countries mostly have a demand for the hospitality industry, or farming which are in high demand. If you have a specific skill, jobs are mostly needed in Sydney/Melbourne or Auckland/Wellington. In these cities you will find hostels marketed at hosting backpackers for monthly rates while they find a job and somewhere to rent. All these cities have local expat magazines that are full of job adverts and places up for rent, so it's very easy to blend into the job and flat hunting crowd when in these cities.

Example of magazine in Australia: www.tntdownunder.com

Outside of these major cities, the jobs are mostly targeted around tourism or farming so if you're happy to work in these areas you can travel around and see what you can find. Otherwise, skill sets are focused towards the major cities.

Once you have found a place and a job and you're all set, you can really enjoy these countries for up to a year. With the money you have saved up during that time, you can even travel around afterwards. It's really an amazing experience to travel half way across the world and set up a new and exciting life for a few years.

It can be tough to find a place to live and get a job but stick at it and make sure you don't waste your whole year of the visa. Sure you're going to miss your family and friends back home but you can make new ones where you are and with Skype you're never more than a phone call away. Stick at it and you will have an adventure for sure. The most amazing thing about it is; as much of an adventure it will be, the culture is very similar to back home so the language and food will help you fit in well. The culture and nightlife is way more fun though, so it will be a top experience with an easy adaptable culture.

Australia vs. New Zealand

Both are very different but yet very similar. I think Australia attracts a different party crowd as it's more focused on the beaches and BBQ culture. New Zealand has more nature in terms of snowy mountains, glaciers, and extreme sports. It also tends to attract a more laid back extreme sports seeking crowd. But both are worth visiting and enjoying in their own rights, so read up on them and see what best suits you.

WARNING once you have applied for your visa you can only get it once, so please choose your time wisely. If you can only work a few months before you fly to somewhere else, you're not making the most out of the full year working visa. Plan your visa wisely and use it when you can to its full. It would be a shame to use it for a month, not pick up any work and then want to do it again two years later when you feel more in the mood. It doesn't work like that, unfortunately you can only apply once and then get it once. The clock is ticking because once you're over 35 you can no longer apply.

Singapore Working Visa

Working in Singapore can last an internship period, which is mostly around 3 months. The difference with this visa is you have to find a job before you start normally within a needed skill area that you are qualified in. For example, I studied a degree in tourism and as hospitality is in demand, I worked at a hotel reception there. Working in Singapore is an incredible opportunity to work in Asia. The language is English and it is widely spoken so there is no barrier with regards to language. Also all the signs and paperwork are in English so it's easy to integrate into the country and its community. The best way to find work is to go through an agency that will have many places on their books and will aim to find a placement to best suit your needs. I used Speedwing (www.speedwing.org) and found them very helpful and easy to use. In fact it made my whole working experience a breeze.

You can also do it yourself by contacting the Ministry of man power, but you must seek employment on your own which might be challenging unless you have something in mind or a highly sort after skill. here is the link if you want to take this option:

www.mom.gov.sg

United States of America

It's extremely difficult to get a working visa in The United States of America. Not only do you have to be in a current job that will transfer you to the USA, the job that you are transferring to needs to be a specific role that only you can fill and no other American can. Comparing this to Australia or New Zealand, why bother with all the hassle, it's much easier to just go there where you can easily apply for a working visa and get it without being in a current job. However there is one alternative:

Camp America

www.campamerica.co.uk

In order to work on a summer camp in the USA you can apply for a J1 visa. This is a lot different to a full working visa as it is specifically targeted at students looking for summer jobs, such as with a summer camp. In the US it's very common to send your kids off to summer camp whilst school is out for the summer. That is why lots of students are hired to look after the kids. This can be an exciting experience as you will be put onto a camp with other similar aged helpers from all over Europe ready to have an awesome summer. You make a lot of friends that you work with and you make loads of friends with the campers as well. If you get on with them really well it's very popular for the parents to invite you over to stay at their place whilst you are travelling around the USA which can be a great cultural experience as American homes can be massive compared to British ones. By the end of the camp, you will have earned enough money to travel around the United States of America, and possibly into Mexico or Canada. Many camp staff get together and buy a rental car to drive along the coast. You will probably turn your adventure into a road trip once the summer work has finished.

Canada Working Visa

www.canadainternational.gc.ca

Pretty much the same culture as in the USA but way more totally awesome. Not only this, but applying for a working visa is a lot more simple than picking up a job in the States. For this reason I would actually recommend going and working in Canada. If you happen to enjoy skiing then this is really an awesome opportunity as you can work during a snow season on one of the resorts. You can work as an instructor, or cleaning rooms, or working the bars for the visitors. Canada is such a large country with lots of different unique places to visit and can be a really fun experience. Compared to working in the US which can be tough to get the visa for Brits, why don't you just work in Canada instead and be awesome?

South Korea - Teaching English

Teaching English can be a fun experience. If you have a university degree that's all you need to apply for a one year English Teaching placement in South Korea. The pay is very good as well and for a new graduate it can really help to pay off those expensive student loans you have weighing on your shoulders. Many other destinations such as Japan or Dubai require a TEFL teaching qualification but South Korea do not require this so if you wanted a fast option towards a well paid job, then this option can be for you.

You can apply through an agency and select what part of South Korea you want to work in. If you have a TEFL qualification, this will affect your employability and total salary offered. If you don't have a TEFL you get paid a little less and if you work outside Seoul you will also be paid less than someone working in the capital city (Roughly high end is around £24,000 per year depending on the agreement you have made). The school will most likely pay for your return flights as well which is normal custom. Other areas which are also covered is your flat, a starter fee so you can buy bedding and cooking equipment. They even pay a completing bonus on finishing. It's also popular that if you do a good job and the school wants to keep you, they will pay you a fee to carry on for an extra year and extend your flights to cater for the new arrangement. Sound too good to be true? It really is, and that's why I recommend South Korea over any other country as they really have a drive to excel on the global stage and feel that good English teachers are the way towards this path so make the most out of this opportunity!

For global teaching opportunities you can look more further here:

www.teachaway.com

Europe

http://ec.europa.eu/social

If you have an EU passport then you can work anywhere within the EU, and I mean anywhere with no restrictions, how amazing an opportunity is that? You can work as a Ski Instructor for British tourists in Austria. You can work on a party resort as a rep in Greece. You can work in a hostel looking after Aussie backpackers in Barcelona. You could work on a campsite cleaning caravans in France. You could pick berries in Norway. Or, how about being a tour guide in Amsterdam? Anything in Europe is possible, so seek out the possibilities.

Studying Abroad

Erasmus program: www.britishcouncil.org/erasmus

How about university? Do you know that as an EU citizen you can do a whole year on exchange in any

EU country (as long as; it's not your final year, the university has a similar course, it is in English, and they are able to exchange ECT credits) all for free through an exchange grant system. Yes it's true, in fact I did it and it was incredible and one of the most amazing experiences of my life. I returned to my university in the UK knowing so much more than when I left, but not only this I made shed loads of incredible friends and experienced what it's like to live and study in another country. Do it if you can! You won't regret it.

What If I told you that you could study abroad for a fraction of the cost compared to in the UK, get taught in English and pretty much get the same degree as well as experiencing living in another country as well as meeting loads of locals and making lots of international friends. It's true. Take the Netherlands for example, they teach many international degrees in English. You can also study for a one year master's and it will cost a fifth of what it does in the UK.

Really look into it, I'm not making this stuff up:

www.studyinholland.nl

But what If I told you that if you were to study in Finland, Sweden, Iceland, Norway or Denmark the tuition fee is free and they also have English courses on offer? How about bloody that! And have I mentioned how awesome all of those countries are to live in? From past experience, they are pretty bloody incredible. So why are you studying in the UK? I hope I at least made you think a little differently.

www.norden.org

Chapter Thirty Two: Wrapping it up

Travel will shape you as a person and there are lessons to be learned. I can offer you three pieces of advice:

Do things that scare you, step out of your comfort zone and don't be afraid to jump.

Learn from your mistakes it will make you a better person than those who never did anything at all.

And make the most out of all opportunities that come your way, they normally only come around once.

This is where I now leave you. It's now up to you to start your own adventure.

Now go and see the world!

About the Author

My name's Dave and for the past 8 years I have been travelling. I got bitten by the travel bug back in 2005 and I haven't stopped since. It's been a crazy journey from then till now, and I'm not thinking about stopping any time soon.

From the age of 15 I have travelled to over 70+ countries, studied and lived in Finland and The Netherlands, worked and lived in Singapore, Switzerland and the USA, and this was all funded on just a shoestring budget.

Not only have I gained all these travelling experiences, I'm qualified as well. I studied travel and tourism for two years at college and then went on to study International Travel and Tourism Management at University. At the moment I'm studying a master's degree in social media at Tilburg University which is another interest of mine.

In my free time I enjoy running my travel blog: www.traveldave.co.uk

Contact the Author

If you enjoyed this book or would like to get in contact with me, feel free; plenty of different ways:

Twitter: @Traveldaveuk

Facebook: www.facebook.com/pages/traveldaveuk

And good old email: dave@traveldave.co.uk

Copyright (c) David Timothy Brett, 2014

All rights reserved.

Printed in Great Britain
by Amazon